Catholics And Their Right To Married Priests

Struggles with the Vatican

Heinz-J. Vogels

Gotham Books

30 N Gould St.
Ste. 20820, Sheridan, WY 82801
https://gothambooksinc.com/

Phone: 1 (307) 464-7800

© 2023 *Heinz-J. Vogels*. All rights reserved.

No part of this book may be reproduced, stored in a retrieval system, or transmitted by any means without the written permission of the author.

Published by Gotham Books (November 9, 2023)

ISBN: 979-8-88775-683-7 (P)
ISBN: 979-8-88775-684-4 (E)

Because of the dynamic nature of the Internet, any web addresses or links contained in this book may have changed since publication and may no longer be valid.

The views expressed in this work are solely those of the author and do not necessarily reflect the views of the publisher, and the publisher hereby disclaims any responsibility for them.

The author: Dr. Heinz-Jürgen Vogels, born in Berlin in 1933, ordained a priest in Cologne in 1959, 1967-1979 research assistant at the Albertus-Magnus-Institute in Bonn, editing the works of Albert the Great, 1974 concluded a sacramental "emergency" marriage with Renate Schwarz before two witnesses, 1975 doctorate in theology in Mainz, 1978 published the book "Compulsory Celibacy", 1979 civil marriage with Renate Schwarz, suspension of his ecclesiastical office, 1983-1985 Head of the Preparatory Commission for the "General Synod of Married Priests and their Wives" held in Ariccia near Rome, from 1986 to 2002 member of the Executive Committee of the "International Federation of Married Catholic Priests".

Publications: "Christ's descent into the realm of the dead" (Christi Abstieg ins Totenreich, doctoral thesis), Freiburg 1976. Co-editor of first volume 1 of the "Summa Theologiae" of Albert the Great, Münster 1978. "Compulsory Celibacy" (Pflichtzölibat), Munich 1978, Bonn 1992. "Jesus Christ – a reality" (Jesus Christus – eine Realität), Ostfildern 1988. Celibacy– Gift or Law? Tunbridge Wells 1992, Kansas City 1993. Discussion with Karl Rahner on christology and trinity (in German), Bonn 2002. Twelve famous misunderstandings of the Catholic Faith (German), Bonn 2005, 2007.

Contents

Preface	*ix*
Introduction	
Chapter 1	
Grace Enhanced the Beginnings	*11*
Chapter 2	
Obligatory Celibacy Makes Sick	*17*
Chapter 3	
The Courage To Jump	*41*
Chapter 4	
The Difficulty Of Walking On Water	*58*
Chapter 5	
A Priest Marries	*71*
Chapter 6	
The Wearing Down Feud	*100*
Chapter 7	
After The Matrimonial Yes - Excommunication	*114*
Chapter 8	
Taking Another Direction	*124*
Chapter 9	
The Mustard Seed Grows Into A Tree	*138*
Chapter 10	
A Victory Of The Right	*146*
Appendix	157

Preface

Catholics worldwide suffer from a dire shortage of priests. The only solution, a commonly shared opinion says, are married priests. A precondition for this to happen is a change of the discipline for priests: They should generally be allowed to be married, if they do not have the charism of living a celibate life – and very few do, according to Matt 19:11.

The sexual abuse crisis, started in Boston in 2002, continued in Ireland a few years later, and in Germany in 2010, likewise draws the attention to the celibacy law. No-one will doubt that at least a good part of sexual abuse by clerics is due to enforced celibacy. Already in 1139, when the Second Lateran Council introduced compulsory celibacy, bishop Ulric of Imola in Italy said: "When celibacy is imposed, priests will commit sins far worse than fornication. Since some men cannot live by the counsel of perfect chastity, they will seek sexual release wherever they can find it" (Anne L. Barstow, Married Priests and the Reforming Papacy – The Eleventh Century Debates, New York 1982, 112).

The calling to the priesthood and the calling to marriage so far exclude each other according to the Roman view, at least in the Western part of the Catholic Church. The rigid enforcement of the celibacy law has its price however. On one hand, ever fewer young men decide to become priests under these circumstances. On the other hand, 95,000 priests worldwide have married since the end of the Second Vatican Council, of whom about 45,000 are still alive.

Heinz-Jürgen Vogels, born in Berlin on 25 May, 1933, was ordained a priest by the Archbishop of Cologne, Cardinal Josef Frings, on February

2, 1959. Vogels contracted a sacramental marriage in 1974, without giving up his priesthood. He wanted to be both: Catholic priest and Catholic husband. Because — as Vogels argues — according to the Bible data in 1 Cor 9:5, preachers of the Gospel have the right "to take along a wife," and this divine right has priority over the current ecclesiastic law.

The records of Heinz-Jürgen Vogels are exciting to read, like a detective story. The author portrays the various and often exhausting stages of his battle against a law which became obsolete long ago. In unrelenting sincerity, the married priest shows to what extent he personally experienced the pathogenic aspects of compulsory celibacy for Catholic clerics, and he reports on how and in what form he found healing through marriage. He was, however, not content to find a solution solely for himself, but right from the outset was anxious to launch his case as an example for the majority of priests, and for the benefit of the communities deprived of a pastor.

This report, placed under the motto: *Deus deducit ad inferos et reducit* (1 Kg 2:6), resembles a psycho-thriller, but what is worst is that it is a true story. At the same time it presents a great deal of general information, on the Bible, church history, church law, as well as psychology. It gives insight in typical Catholic behaviour and tradition.

To understand how dates and words could be remembered to such an exact extent: minutes were recorded from memory immediately after conversations, and the whole story has been drafted in various sections since 1965, once every five years, without knowing how life would go on. And it is still a story with an open end, an objective not yet reached: Full acknowledgement of a married priesthood in the Western Catholic Church.

Bible texts are quoted from The Revised English Bible with Apocrypha (Oxford University Press, 1989), at some instances corrected by the author to be nearer to the Greek text.

Some final remarks: The suffering described in some early chapters are now over and forgotten. Yet readers can see how difficult it is to get truth acknowledged. Finally, however, as reported in chapters 8-10, the Vatican up to the highest ranks and even Cardinal Ratzinger, had to issue approving statements, which justify the publication of this report. Consistency is lacking: That the Vatican acts according to what its officials have said.

Introduction

Alone Against the Vatican

Location of the act: Campo Santo in Rome. – Date: 12 October, 1974. – Two men meet for a conversation in the world's capital of the Roman Catholic Church. One is a priest, the other his superior.

Their topic is somewhat delicate. It is celibacy. Or better, the obligation to live as celibate, which the church imposes on its priests.

A Priest Fights For His Right To Marry

The priest believes – like many other Catholics – that the law on celibacy practised for centuries should finally be amended and that the church should leave it up to the priests themselves to judge whether they would like to live as celibates or not. Even more so, the priest is absolutely convinced that the church has no right at all legally to require celibacy of its priests, but that priests – on the contrary – have a right to get married.

For the Bible itself provides explicit evidence that Christian clergy have the right to be married. "Do we not have the right," the apostle Paul writes in his first letter to the Corinthians, "to take along a sister in faith as a wife, just like the other apostles and the brothers of the Lord, and like Kephas?" (1 Cor 9:5). The priest in his argument comes back to this verse from the Bible time and time again.

The priest's superior, however, sees things a little differently, to say the least. In his function as General Vicar – i.e. as the representative of the bishop responsible for the priest, in this case Cologne's Archbishop Cardinal

Höffner - he pleads for the point of view of the official church. And this point of view is quite clear and unequivocal: Priests cannot marry.

The priest, however, is not only convinced that priests can marry, but has already acted on that conviction. He has married. More precisely, the priest has contracted a sacramental marriage with a woman he loves dearly. This marriage took place, he is convicted, totally in concordance with current church law. On legal grounds, the priest believes this marriage should therefore be acknowledged as a valid marriage, including by the church itself. But, the church has refused to do just this so far. Therefore, the priest has pressed to have this conversation at the Campo Santo.

"What do you actually want?" asks the General Vicar of the Cologne diocese.

"Have not you read my letters to the Cardinal?" replies the priest.

"Yes, I have read them," the Cardinal's representative answers.

"Then you will know," says the priest, "that I can neither live in the priesthood alone nor in marriage alone, but that I have eventually reached the conclusion that I have the calling to priesthood and marriage".

"Prior to your ordination, you completely and voluntarily, after mature consideration, accepted the condition required by the Latin Church to remain celibate, and you even asked for the ordination," the General Vicar replies, "this follows from the records..."

The conversation between the priest of the archdiocese Cologne and his superior at the Campo Santo in Rome lasts nearly forty-five minutes. It begins at 14.30, and ends at 15.15. More of it is contained in Chapter 5 below. Eleven years later – again in the neighbourhood of the capital of the Roman Catholic Church – an event takes place which deals with the same problems.

In August 1985, the so-called "General Synod of Married Catholic Priests and their Wives", met in Ariccia near Rome. At this internationally frequented forum, the question was discussed of whether the sacrament of ordination and the sacrament of marriage are compatible. As could be expected, the answer is a clear yes. In a unanimous declaration, the compatibility of the sacraments of priesthood and marriage is stated and underpinned with theological arguments.

"The married Catholic priests represented in this synod and their wives," thus the wording of the declaration, unanimously give testimony "on the basis of the church's decisions on faith," to the authorisation of the apostles and all the preachers of the gospel, attested in the first Letter to the Corinthians, "to take along a sister in faith as a wife into the communities" (1 Cor 9:5), an authorisation which belongs to the invariable divine right that cannot be abrogated by the church legislator and is moreover a fundamental human right.

This declaration, printed in full wording in the appendix to this book, is signed by Giustino Zampini, president of the synod, by the co-president, Bishop Jerónimo Podestà from Argentina, by Paolo Camellini, the secretary of the Synod, and by me – Heinz-Jürgen Vogels, the coordinator of the meeting.

This "General Synod of Married Catholic Priests and their Wives" marked an important phase in the decades of battle on which I will report in the following autobiographical records.

The priest just mentioned, who on that autumn day in October 1974 had a discussion with the then General Vicar of Cologne, Peter Nettekoven, at the Campo Santo in Rome and tried to convince him with his arguments, was also myself. In 1974, I, as a priest in office, entered into a sacramental marriage with Renate Schwarz before two witnesses, i.e. without the assistance of a priest and without having received dispensation from Rome for this marriage.

Church law provides such a form of emergency marriage in mission countries, where a priest, entitled to bless marriages, can only visit once every six months. Yet an emergency is also given if not only an exterior – so-called physical – impossibility exists to call a priest, but also, if a moral impossibility is given to have a priest assist at one's marriage. It is the couple itself which, according to Catholic teaching, mutually gives the sacrament, not the priest, who merely "assists" at the wedding ceremony.

Calling in a priest would have been morally impossible for us in 1974, because every priest knows that the law on celibacy still exists, a law that prohibits any priest from marrying and even makes marriage legally impossible for him. We, my wife and I, however, had the long proven conviction that the biblical "right of the apostles to take along a wife," invoked by Paul in 1 Cor 9:5, as a *'ius divinum'* is stronger than the church's ban on marrying. Just like in the German legal system, constitutional law precedes and breaks federal law and the law of the federal states, the divine right of the Sacred Scripture precedes and breaks the merely ecclesiastical law, according to Catholic teaching. Therefore we appealed to the emergency rite of marriage for ourselves and got married in the presence of two witnesses.

At the time, the fact that I was not immediately suspended from office and from the priesthood, but was allowed to work as a priest for five more years, despite my sacramental marriage, i.e. as a Catholic priest of the Western Church, without having been dispensed from the celibacy law, already marked a victory.

My wife and I had promised not to practise our marriage as long as no decision had been taken on the validity of our marriage. However, it took many long years before such a decision was taken - admittedly in indirect form, but nevertheless through church law itself. The Vatican, which I, in due form and through all church court instances, had asked for a decision on our sacramental marriage, finally made it known to me that it "does not want to make a judgment," because it did not want to decide on the underlying Bible verse 1 Cor 9:5. With this very statement, however, I believe our marriage – a Catholic priest wedding -, had been declared valid, because the "Codex Iuris Canonici" – the Code, in which the law valid in the Roman Catholic church is established – contains the following regulation regarding marriage: "Marriage enjoys the protection of the law (*gaudet favore iuris*), therefore in case of doubt, one must adhere to the validity of the marriage until the opposite is proven " (Codex Iuris Canonici, edition of 1983, can. 1060). The Vatican did not want to prove the opposite. Since the Vatican undoubtedly knows this canon, it was without doubt aware of the consequences of its unwillingness to reach a decision. Our marriage is to be regarded valid.

So, it seems I had contracted a valid marriage as a Catholic priest on the basis of the biblical right of priests to marry, according to 1 Cor 9:5, which the Vatican did not want to or could not declare null and void. If not even the Vatican, the highest authority in the Catholic church, wanted to bring an action against the validity of our marriage, which it must do according to the law, then nobody can apparently "prove the opposite" of the validity, hence our marriage is valid according to current ecclesiastical law.

Consequently, it is plain to be seen for all who want to see. Priests have an apostolic right to live in wedlock, but the Vatican "does not want" to acknowledge this right.

Priests Can Marry

Some 20% of Catholic priests live in matrimony. However, the figure does not include former priests, nor those, who have been officially dismissed from church service and had to retire due to their non-compliance with the law on celibacy, but priests, who actually do perform service in the church. Besides those priests who are allowed to be married on the basis of a dispensation, because they formerly belonged to another denomination, where they were married, and after their transition to the Catholic church may continue to be married without having to give up their marriage, it is above all the priests of the originally Catholic Churches of Eastern rite, for instance in Hungary, the Czech Republic, or Ukraine, in Lebanon or in India, who are married and hold office as priests. They work under the authority of the Pope just like the priests of the Western Church, but can be married with his blessing.

The Roman Catholic Church therefore applies double standards. While it still demands a celibate life from its own priests, the priests of the Uniate Churches of Eastern rite can marry without any problems. This is a legal contradiction within the same church, which should not be there; and we must wonder in all seriousness how the Pope can bless the Eastern rite priests, who are married, with one hand, while with the other, he dispels the priests of the Western Church as soon as they marry?

The claim for the right of priests to live in wedlock is often misunderstood as a demand for the total abolition of celibacy. What it is actually all about, however, is not abolishing celibacy, but rather only about finally letting go of the unjust and unjustifiable celibacy law, and of restoring the truly "Catholic", i.e., the all-encompassing fullness in the real sense of the word. The apostles had already shown that both possibilities exist in the church: the celibacy *and* marriage of a community leader. Peter was married, Paul not. Both were outstanding apostles, both left to the Church of Rome their apostolic authority. Both should also express themselves in its legislation and in its life.

At the moment, priests who are married are marked, especially in official documents of the official church, as "unfaithful", "fallen" or "failed", e.g.

in Pope Paul VI's encyclical of 1967 *Sacerdotalis caelibatus*. Yet, married priests have not become disloyal to their calling to the priesthood, but have rather followed their calling to another state of life, in obedience towards God. The aim of my autobiographical report is to show and prove, on the basis of my own case, that there are indeed different callings within the priesthood, the calling to celibacy and the calling to matrimony.

Celibacy Is Not Good For All

The ability to live a celibate life is "not given ... to all," according to a saying by Jesus (see Matt 19:11), and therefore celibacy is not good for all. Since the findings made by Sigmund Freud and Carl Gustav Jung, the human sciences have shown what it looks like in humans who have to suppress their sexuality, because they are obliged to observe celibacy without having been called to it. As a rule, they become neurotic, depressed, unhappy in their loneliness (Louise Haggett, The Bingo Report, Freeport ME 2005), or are tempted to abuse adults and minors. In fact, they become neurotic, because they suppress what must develop: namely the ability to love, the God given dependence on the completion by a partner.

God is not a rival of the human partner, he does not replace the woman at the side of the celibate man, but God is the goal of love for each and every human being. Therefore, he cannot heal the deficit either, which the prohibition of human partnership produces in those who have been forced to live as celibates.

The fact that many priests, despite prayer, despite receiving the sacraments, and despite tough self-discipline, have become neurotics or were unable to fulfil their assumed obligations is proven by practice. Many doctors, psychologists and therapists can tell a sad story of this. Even the Vatican authorities must acknowledge the inability of many priests to remain celibate, because the authorities have to issue so many dispensations from celibacy. The fact that neuroses in the opinion of most psychoanalytic schools are prepared by mental injuries in earliest childhood, is no argument against this inability of priests (for a lack of charisma from God). If legally imposed celibacy obstructs the way to marriage, the neurotic bases must get even more rigid. The effort spent on permanently repressing can otherwise turn completely normal and emotionally healthy people neurotic, if they do not possess the "charisma" of celibacy, that is, if the special gift of celibacy has not been given to them by God.

From this point of view, therefore, it is possible to split priests into two groups. On one hand, there are those "charismatics" who have been enabled by God to live in celibacy; they will be healthy, resting in themselves, mature and – despite some interior battles – content with their celibacy, because they have received the gift of God (1 Cor 7:7), which enables them to live this life. Other priests, however, and their number is increasing, must state that they do not receive the gift of "eunuch" (Matt 19:12), despite persistent prayer, but possibly become sick, restricted, or obstructed in their effectiveness, because such a central function of life as the longing for intimate partnership and the compulsion to pass on life cannot be suppressed without severe consequences. The Roman poet, Horatius, already aptly said: "You may drive out nature with the pitchfork, but it will nevertheless come back" (nátur(am) éxpellas furcá, tamen úsque recúrret, Horiatius, Epistle I,10,24).

Those who want to escape the consequences of becoming or remaining sick will break out from the constraints of the law in one way or another, either in secret, as the great French pulpit speaker, Bishop Jacques-Bénigne Bossuet (1627-1704), the most famous example did, or publicly, as those priests, who sought dispensation from the law, have done so since 1964 in ever increasing numbers.

Painful Experiences

My own painful experiences seem to me to be an example of how the celibacy law can drive a man and his priestly calling into the ground. If I publicise the story of my "odd illness", as my bishop, Cologne's cardinal Josef Frings called it, as well as the consequences of that "church originated neurosis," which the psychoanalysts stated as their diagnosis, I do so, because I hope to do the fellow believers in the church a service. For, what happened in me, probably occurs in similar form in the souls of other priests and seminarians, as well.

The first part of my report, especially, resembles the story of a sick man. And that it was. I want to show how a so-called ecclesiogenic neurosis develops, that is, a mental disturbance caused by the church, an inhibition in the psychic development on the basis of specifically church-related reasons. It is, however, also my intention to uncover the deeper reasons for the incapacity of so many priests to uphold the celibacy requirement. The obligation to live in celibacy is too much for many, because not all have received the charisma of celibacy. Only those who by grace *"can* grasp it"

(Matt 19:12), will in fact be able to grasp it, and those who do not grasp it, i.e. those who are not able to live in celibacy, because they did not receive the divine gift required for this, will become sick, despite all their good will and endeavours and despite all their prayers.

The individual priest bears no responsibility for this illness, for nobody can be obliged to do something of which they are not capable, for the lack of a particular grace of God. "*Ultra posse nemo tenetur*", nobody can be obliged to exceed their own resources, this is a principle of Christian morality. An error on the part of the Catholic Western Church, which has continued for centuries, namely that marriage makes "impure" is responsible for the illness. The law on celibacy was justified in 1139 with the following reasoning: "To spread the *purity*, which pleases God, among priests, we determine that married bishops and priests shall be separated," thus stated in Canon 7 of the Second Council of the Lateran! "Ut … Deo placens *munditia* in sacris ordinibus dilatetur, statuimus… quatenus … separentur": Conciliorum Oecumenicorum Decreta, Bologna 1957, p.174.

The heart of the problem can be summarised in these simple terms. The law on celibacy originated from the church's interest in the cultic purity of priests, no longer acknowledged today as a solid reason. Therefore, church leaders can no longer with good reason, nor in good faith, demand from all priests a celibate way of life, because a charisma is needed to live in celibacy, a gift which is not given to all priests. Without that charisma, celibacy can result in leaving the ministry, or abuse, or sickness.

That is what has happened to me. When, as young man in the seminary, I prepared myself for my future profession, I wanted to become a priest with such commitment, because I felt called by God, that I believed celibacy "must just be possible." But, after I had been ordained a priest on 2 February, 1959, I fell into a deep depression from which I was finally freed with the help of physicians and, in October 1960, through a pilgrimage to the shrine of Mary in Kevelaer, near the Dutch border. I became aware that my body and soul had responded to the excessive demands of the celibacy law with a depressive "reflex of behaving as if dead," just as animals do when threatened with extreme danger. On returning from Kevelaer, I took with me the relief that it was not God who demanded celibacy from me, but only the church.

And so began the decades of my battle against the Western Church's demand for celibacy. Luckily, I was able to achieve a strange victory in 1987, that is, the Vatican's implicit acknowledgement of my marriage, as reported above.

If I begin the portrayal of this battle with a retrospective on my childhood, it is because only through this view of my completely healthy and normal childhood will it be possible to understand that my difficulties with celibacy, caused by the law, are not rooted in my childhood, but stem from outside, from the circumstances, or to use the technical terms: were exogenous and not endogenous factors. In other words, that I became sick through celibacy, but had not already been sick before.

Chapter 1
Grace Enhanced the Beginnings

A strange relationship exists between Pope Gregory VII and myself. It was exactly this pope, who, in the Middle Ages, did most to enforce celibacy, and whom the church has, since 1606, venerated as a saint, had his feast on the very day I saw the light of day. Was he going to repair an error by protecting me?

Childhood In Berlin

My birthday marked two fests. In 1933, the date May 25 not only marked the anniversary of Pope Gregory VII, but that year also celebrated Christ's Ascension on the same day. I was baptised in the Franziskus Hospital. I was the youngest in our family. My siblings were five and four years older. We grew up in the big rooms of our apartment in Berlin-Zehlendorf, with Berlin's famously long "corridor". In front of our flat, the National Road No. 1 passed through, the "Berliner Straße" and "Potsdamer Straße", which led from Koenigsberg in East-Prussia through Duesseldorf to Aachen, more than a thousand kilometres through the German countryside, connecting it with the adjoining countries.

It was just a short walk to the primary school through the villas of our suburb, where each street had lovely lawns with trees and garden hedges. The parish church was likewise not far away, a Heart of Jesus Church, in an as warm and red brick-Gothic style as you can find elsewhere in the Margrave of Brandenburg, as the style of the Monastery of Chorin and St Mary's Church in Prenzlau.

My father had the position of a Ministerial Director (Ministerialdirigent) at the Department of Justice. He died early, aged 53, on March 6, 1942, during a short vacation in the Alps. Only later did I become aware of how much he must have suffered under the way the Nazis treated the "law". This was probably why he travelled so often into the mountains over his last few years. In his diaries, I found the entry that he had left a meeting with lawyers and state officials, "because these men had too little reverence for the German Civil Code," which had been in force since 1870.

There was hardly anybody, after his death, who would have spoken badly about him. "Against a world of enemies," as he recounted to our mother, he had in 1939 defended the handwritten last will and testament of the individuals, in his project of a bill, against the totalitarian state, who wanted to subdue citizens in that respect, too, and he had asserted its realisation. After the war, this "Wills Act" (Testaments Gesetz), was adopted as an integral part of the German Civil Code. Thus, at least one of his works for the freedom of humankind, when they face their death, lives on, even after the end of the Nazi regime.

School Days In Wartime

In 1943, after all the families with children had been evacuated from Berlin, my brother and I were sent to the Joachimsthalsches Gymnasium in Templin, a grammar school of the old humanist hallmark. However, this only remained true for half a year, and then the spectre of Nazi rule tried to enter there, too. Initially, we did not notice too much, we were too young, myself ten years old, and too well founded. The farmers' sons from Mecklenburg-Western Pomerania stemmed from families which tended to be positioned on the side of the opposition. I, myself, did not really understand what it was all about. Latin, mathematics, later on Greek, could poorly be filled with the spectre of Nazi rule for young grammar school students. I had been an altar boy in Berlin and had perceived such happiness at the altar, near the sanctuary, that nothing could have detracted me from these values. Just before the evacuation from Berlin, I had been received, together with other boys of the same age, into the Catholic parish youth, secretly meeting in the basement of the rectory, where rooms had been made available for youngsters; an experience, which filled us with immense respect for the "old ones", strong characters of the Catholic youth movement, and had shown us the obligations and the pride of belonging to them.

The war put a sudden end to the children's school day idyll. My brother had to join a kind of "home guard", the ('Volkssturm') on the nearby front, even at the end of April 1945, just eight days before the end of the war, right on his sixteenth birthday. Luckily, he survived after soon incurring a minor injury. On the same day, my mother took me back with her to the property of an aunt near Prenzlau.

The Desire to Be In The Church Like Outside

After the war had come to an end, school in Berlin began without delay in May 1945. I joined the class in September. I only want to give a few indicators to show how rich and full of life these years were, how intact my relationship with Father God and my life in the church, in other words, to give an impression of what was later destroyed.

I learned to play the violin with great joy, I sang in the school choir and also had my place in the student orchestra and in the school theatre. The other circle of life was the parish and its youth. How serious were the discussions we had during the evening meetings in the basement of the rectory, what a deep feeling of community! Later on, I led a group of youngsters. I saw and felt myself as healthy, strong, receiving and giving, loved and loving.

What I owe the community in the parish youth groups cannot easily be measured. The Heart of Jesus Church was "home and paternal house," as our 'foreman', fatherless like myself, always called it. The chaplain, a true man, with his sermons touched the bottom of our souls. He placed before our eyes God's "unbelievable" deeds with us human beings time and time again. But the patriarchal, always constant dignity of the parish priest, too, played a part in founding a solid faith in us.

A tender, reverential, just budding love transformed the last two years before I gained my grammar school leaving certificate. It developed with the sister of a boy, whom I had to help in his school work for Greek. One day, the parents also asked me to give his sister a few lessons. The small female foot slowly moved under the table towards mine, while I held my head bent over the Greek grammar. Then, two glances met which were no longer those of teacher and student. Under the eyes of both parents, a spring developed in autumn and its golden colours reflected in our faces. They never had enough of looking at each other.

The girlfriend was a Protestant, as most schoolmates and the Berlin environment were. We Catholics lived in the so-called Diaspora and this preserved us from acquiring any denominational arrogance. We grew up in the awareness of a shared Christianity, in which Catholics admittedly believed they were living in the centre and in the fullness. However, we took care not to admit any thought of proselytism and respected the human qualities of "others", at least as much as that of our fellow believers. I remember that a conversation with her about the question, "Do we not all believe in the same God?" satisfied me most deeply; we had this conversation while standing between the jaws of the sandy Grunewald.

The programme that I had slowly developed for my life was this. To be and to behave in the church just like outside, and outside just like in the church; that is, in the area of the sanctuary as natural as in everyday life, and in the course of the day as faithful as during the church service. This could, of course, not be achieved without concessions, but I think I was on the way towards this goal.

God's Irresistible Calling

In the words of Theodor Heuss, the first President of the Federal Republic of Germany, the German grammar school leaving certificate, the "Abitur", marks the time of the broadest general formation of a human being in our days, which will never again be achieved. The end of my grammar school days also meant separation from my home town of Berlin with its great dimensions, its cultural wealth, in artistic perfection, its cosmopolitanism, its political vigilance and its strong mother-wit. It was as if a plant had been removed from its maternal mould, into which it was interwoven with so many roots.

The departure from Berlin did not happen voluntarily at all. Half a year earlier, my mother had already moved into the new Federal capital, Bonn, so I had to follow, no matter what. I began to study law in my father's footprints. My mother's predecessors, too, had been judges through four generations. The professors in Bonn, who still had good memories of my father from the negotiations between science and the ministerial bureaucracy, told me how much esteem they had held for him. But the legal thinking had not really touched me in my guts.

A year after leaving grammar school, I felt God's irresistible calling to the priesthood. In my last year in Berlin, when I lived alone in our apartment and later with friends, on one evening – after our youth group had discussed what occupations the friends might one day take up, a thought already came to my mind. Actually, only the chaplain does anything of meaning. He labours for eternity, points to it before the people and worries that as many as possible arrive from where he bears witness. Isn't that the only occupation worth taking up? All others, even if necessary, are of limited sense and limited duration.

In the meantime, I had given law a try. Professors had affirmed that I had grasped the legal thinking. It should later on be most useful for me, also in the church. In the afternoon and evening, I could not stay at home long, once more I "had to" take on responsibility for a youth group in the Bonn parish. My sense of being obliged to become active in this area was so strong that I soon developed the same drive at the new domicile as in Berlin – and even became scout leader in the deanery, thus taking on greater responsibility.

The Calling Sheds Much Light

The Easter vigil of 1952 was the first in which the liturgy of Holy Saturday was allowed to be celebrated, as in the early times of Christianity, during the night (not on Saturday mornings), according to the reforms of Pope Pius XII. During this liturgy, in which I took part as a thurifer and lector at the altar, I sensed a strange fulfilment of my whole self with great, cogent clearness. I felt heaven had become closer. It became clear to me in my deepest soul that this is my place, near the altar, at the service of the word of God and the liturgy, and nowhere else.

In this night, I was overwhelmed by such a certainty that God wanted me as a priest, that in the subsequent days I had the perception of not being able to pray "Thy will be done" in the Our Father, if I refused to become a priest.

Only from this experience is it possible to understand why and how I could survive at all during the subsequent years of my studies. I think anyone who should have experienced what I was to live through would surely have drawn the conclusion: "Here you will become sick, you are no longer yourself, you don't belong here!". I stayed on my path, however, despite all, for the rocket's "blast-off" had taken place with such inner force and such shining light that it carried me over the threshold of priesthood, yet only to drop me burnt out immediately after that.

Tears During The Easter Vigil

During this Easter night, full of light, after the end of the liturgy, I wandered through the streets, still glowing from inside. I could not sleep, nor could I communicate with anyone at this stage either. Suddenly, from a bright, truly beaming interior heaven, I got a crying cramp. It was the violent emotion that grasped me at the idea – that from now on I was no longer allowed to marry!

I had not been aware, at the time, of the reasons for the cramp, but can make sense of it today. I remember, however, that I first felt an invincible impulse to cry, and only in the following days, with the clearer realisation of the renunciation that was demanded from me, did I wander around, shadowed with darkness, ready to renounce everything, yet continuously tending to tears, because – for the sake of priestly vocation – I had to accept the renunciation of marriage, which I had seen from a distance only, having a girlfriend in school, but had anticipated as so delightful. I had to renounce, otherwise I would not have been able to pray the Our Father.

Chapter 2
Obligatory Celibacy Makes Sick

I entered the Bonn Seminary. From now on, my life turned inwards. Battles and victories, interests, love and longings, but realisations also took place inwards, in the religious area, instead of outside, where life became constantly poorer. The tree flaked off as in autumn and became repellently bald in the eyes of those who wished me well. My violin playing became ever worse, I had the impression of not being able to speak, the desire to die already appeared during the summer 1953, for months I could not learn anything, however was able, shortly before the end of the term, to sit my exams with a grade of good or even better.

Going Downhill

My personal education impoverished, I did not read any literature, no newspapers, heard and saw little of what happened in the world around me. Yet I maintained contact with my youth group, even if the seminary director did not like it. Nobody can describe the battles fought out in the seminary chapel during the evenings. It was painful that I did not know at all what I actually lacked, and with what I had to fight. Nevertheless, I knew that I had to survive. And there were, of course, also great joys: in the liturgy and in the community of the students in which I lived, particularly in the fraternity of theologians, to which I had affiliated and who were recruited by former group leaders of the Catholic Youth.

Besides, all the negative phenomena only appeared step by step. A revealing symptom for the reason of my depression was the joy I felt in receiving an answer from my girlfriend in Berlin to my first and almost unique letter since the new calling. I had written, in my letter to her, that after all we were living under the same sun and needed not to treat each other as non-existent.

Similarly symptomatic were the freshness and the energy with which I returned to the Seminary from a skiing vacation in the winter of 1953, the first after the war. I had recovered not only through wind and sun over the snow, but also through the shine on the faces of girls, who were likewise on vacation there. We went together on skiing tours and celebrated New Year's Eve.

I didn't know why these vacations had given me so much. Only much later did I recognise the true reason. I was allowed, for a moment, to see again what had been withdrawn from me, without my suspecting, however, that I lacked exactly what I had given up and had believed to be obliged to and also to be able to abstain from: the other half of humankind. So, it continued for four semesters up to the intermediate exams. Then, I was released to Munich for two semesters outside the seminary.

In Munich, I found lodgings with our former neighbours from Berlin. The cordial atmosphere was beneficial for me. They were, in turn, aghast at how "narrow-minded" I had meanwhile become — and indeed I had. I had justified my plea for leave to Munich among others with the reason that I would need the semester outside the seminary "to expand my view". The Seminary director couldn't but laugh: that from a Berliner!

However, I indeed needed one and a half months before I could get a grip on my freedom and on myself again. Then, string quartet playing and other cultural hobbies revived, I went mountain climbing, tower jumping in the swimming pool and became newly interested in literature and politics.

At the university, I could drink from the "living waters" of theology in full draughts and in one term I attended three seminar courses at a time, besides the many lectures. Nevertheless, I felt an inner rupture: an unknown fear paralysed my faith in God.

"I Have A Strange Illness..."

Immediately after the time in Munich, my Bonn student corporation organised a trip to the Holy Land. I had immense profit from it. I summarised it in the words: "We must now believe only half of our faith;

the rest of what is written in the sacred scripture, we have seen: places, names and landscapes, Bethlehem and Jerusalem; it is just like the scripture writes!" The daily contact, however, with the celibate brothers once again brought up that sort of subconscious doubt of myself in me again: It seemed I could not meet the requirements of the church for the priesthood in a crucial point. Thus, even these five weeks were not untroubled.

And so it occurred that the director of the seminary, at the end of my studies, said to me: "You could have done much more in your studies!" Yet, all my desire to study more had been scuppered by my physical and mental incapability, which allowed me to do no more than just the necessary. If this state is compared with the versatility and activity, with the ease of learning before beginning my theology studies, it seems to be almost incredible. I could hardly believe it myself, but had to accept it and to learn to become modest.

Sometimes, I held on to the words of St Paul only: "I did not want to know anything but Jesus Christ, and him as crucified" (1 Cor 2:2). I thought to have this knowledge. On another occasion, I wrote to my former girlfriend in Berlin: "I have a strange illness: I cannot think, and you can imagine what this means for a human being, who is to work with his head." And to my mother, I said: "It will probably take a long time before I find a doctor for *this* kind of illness." I still did not know what was wrong with me. Sometimes, I blamed the bad, humid climate in Bonn for this, but climate alone could not be it. For at that time I didn't feel much better anywhere else.

An Increasing Loss Of Reality

As the senior of the last class, I had to give the farewell speech to the seminary, and it was – for my taste – spiced with humour. Only the unexpectedly sharp reaction by the director and the student community made me aware of how far I had already been driven from reality and how much I lacked a sense of understanding for what effect my words might have. This experience made me humble and resulted, above all, in me remaining at the seminary for one more semester – a fact which reconciled the director – and which gave me the opportunity to begin a theological thesis. I normally would not have had such an idea. The spiritual director, a man of wit, humour and kindliness, had told us about St Don Bosco, namely that he would have made a first class doctorate, but for the sake of his vocation to care for the youth he had abstained from it. I, however, had to fill out my time now. So, I asked a professor for a subject for a thesis.

If I had not begun with this thesis, I would not have gained the scientific equipment necessary later on for the foundation of my thesis on the sacraments of priesthood and marriage being compatible, which probably won the thesis its widespread acknowledgment. The spiritual director in Bonn had already commented at that time: "Who knows, for what it was good, it definitely has a meaning!"

The Narrow Gate

Each Christian must someday pass through the "narrow gate" (Matt 7:13), of which Jesus speaks in his sermon of the mount. Usually, it is illness, misery, need, or the mystic night, prosecution by enemies or friends. For me, this gate appeared to me like a long hose, as a "dark canyon" (Ps 23:4), through which I had to go – a path, along which I, in accordance with the Bible verse of the "narrow path" (Matt 7:14), felt "pressed", as one better could translate the word "narrow".

At the Great Seminary of Bensberg and Cologne reserved for the last two years before ordination, I increasingly had the feeling of being isolated from the outside world; even the brothers seemed to me to live elsewhere. I noticed, although powerless against it, how much I became even more unrealistic and uncertain about myself. At the same time, I felt "inner joy about God's law," as is said in the letter to the Romans (Rom 7:22). The service at the altar was always a great experience and caused a feeling of proximity with God and of community with the brothers. I did not lose the awareness of being called to the priesthood; just the opposite, in fact: this awareness, which had to undergo the toughest personal and exterior control, was strengthened even more. But I felt alienated from myself.

I took part with body and soul in the lecture on mystics. Contrary to the other seminarians, who seemed to be bored and looking around in conversation, because they could find little in the discourse of the professor, I was able to follow the lecture with the utmost attention, because I saw in these explications on the "night of the senses", the "feeling of God", the "spiritual bridal state", the "night of the spirit" and the "mystic marriage", a possible interpretation of my experiences, which strengthened me and equipped me with new strength to survive.

Crying Fits And A Longing For The Altar

Before ordination to the subdeaconate, to which at that time the obligation of celibacy was linked, my severe doubts once more began to take hold of me. They had been prepared for some time. When we sung the evening prayer of Christmas Day, the vespers, when all the seminarians were prepared for the trip home to their families, I felt the desire in me, which I immediately pushed aside, the longing: "Oh, if only my girlfriend in Berlin could pick me up here," just like some brothers were picked up at the seminar by their families. Not for a second did this thought remain in my mind, I immediately suppressed it. Therefore, it was, a few minutes later, completely incomprehensible to me as to why I should get such an irresistible crying fit. I could not battle against it with all my forces. My sobbing could not be kept back. I had to leave the chapel. In the sacristy, I could let it go for some few moments.

Now, the confused seminarian knew even less what to do with himself. I spoke with the seminary director and voluntarily consulted a doctor, who during my studies in Bonn had already given me advice and help. But because neither I nor the doctor could conclude, from where the crying fits originated, he could, at this stage, say little about the diagnosis and just as little about the therapy. It seemed best to pause another semester.

During this time, the thesis again offered an opportunity for activity. What was so strange, was the fact that my intellect seemed to be intact. I could talk well with anyone who should give an opinion about me. But immediately after that, I again fell into brooding, the fears and the feeling of inferiority returned.

Nevertheless, the longing for the altar, where "the sparrow finds a home and a nest the dove" (Ps 84:4), became so strong again that I re-registered at the beginning of the following semester and held on until ordination in February 1959. The doctors were of the opinion that nothing would seem to indicate that I should not be ordained.

Mishaps At The First Mass

Michel Quoist writes in his Prayers "Lord, here I am," commenting on the "prayer of a priest on a Sunday evening," many theologians concentrate their whole concern on their self-perfection, and this "circling around oneself" is often supported by their educators. The essence and task of priestly service is, however, to be found in *love*, in dedicating oneself to the brothers and sisters of Christ. Admittedly, our spiritual director at the seminary pointed to this: in the service of the faithful, the secular priest finds sanctification. But the atmosphere of the house, which necessarily turns the view inside, and my own advanced encapsulation, made it impossible for me to go from the seminar as a loving person.

After my ordination to the deaconate, I had, together with a friend, whom I knew from boy scout times, organised a "missionary meeting", to which we had invited priests from missionary countries, who studied in Rome, to come to Germany for three weeks. My intellectual abilities had been sufficient for that task, while the organisational management lay in the hands of my friend. Nevertheless, this may have induced my superiors to proceed to my ordination, despite all the scruples which little by little might have come to their mind as well.

When our Cardinal and Archbishop Josef Frings laid his hands on us and I still so clearly sensed my insufficiency, I had only the one intention in heart and mouth: to love, to love, to love, that is to give. And yet, I was not capable of it. The following celebration with the family already did not go well, because I had not been able to point the relatives to the right restaurant. Some wandered around and only found us much later. The first Mass on the next morning started half an hour late, because I had given priority to my plans to start, that very same day, on my certainly necessary vacations, not however to the relatives and friends and the parish priest, who were waiting for me in the home parish.

Under circumstances like these, the solemn First Mass on the subsequent Sunday could not be filled with much more spirituality. Only at the end laid I the First Benediction with great love and perseverance on the heads of those kneeling. Here, for the first time, I sensed something of that overpowering, warming love which flows through a priest, when he blesses in God's name. "*Sacerdotem enim oportet benedicere* – a priest is obliged to bless," we had heard in the rite of ordination. This last of the priestly duties, blessing, I was able to fulfil right from the beginning. For the others, I was not yet properly able at that time, because – as Thomas of Aquin puts it – "the grace presupposes nature". One has become very sceptical today, in view of that sentence from the Middle Ages. In my case, however, it finds its confirmation: my nature was weakened; I could not rely on it.

Breakdown Of All Resources

Soon, my health resources dried out completely. At the parish in Cologne-Bayenthal, where I had to give my first service, I was soon unable to withstand a school lesson of catechism – and that, although I had not previously had the slightest difficulties in contact with boys during my scouting activities. Here, however, I could not impose myself, never finished the subject, and finally was not even able to distribute magazines to the altar boys. I couldn't, I did not know how to.

While preparing a sermon, the first part turned out good, as long as I still overlooked the total of the planned explanation, then however my thoughts suddenly stayed away, I could not remember what I was aiming for, and with the best will in the world did not bring the planned ideas to an end. So, I stumbled to the pulpit, with a reasoned start and a vague end.

Each of the daily tasks, even the smallest, required an unspeakable effort. Everything appeared to me like an immense mountain, which to work through took hours. I spent more than a whole afternoon on the question of which songs would be good for the school Mass the next morning. I increasingly allowed myself less sleep, whereby the condition became even worse. I did not dare to eat much more than nothing, was often in church long before Mass began, and yet dragged myself through the prayers with a dry mouth.

Of symptomatic importance was also the fact that since the spiritual exercises before the ordination, I could only say my breviary silently. Previously, I had always said the prayers with low voice. Suddenly, I could only could "read" the breviary.

In this condition of inability, I believed myself lost, hopeless and rejected. The parish priest could no longer stand to see me in this condition at the main altar, and sent me to the side altar. And it was true, my aspect must have been unbearable for the community. Only when distributing the sacred communion did I become a little quieter for a while: if I had nothing to hope for myself, at least I could communicate the salvation and God's love to others.

On The Edge Of Suicide

The despair was a disease, the thoughts of suicide originated from my mental constitution, from which I saw no way out and found my physical strength exhausted. Only years later was I able to recognise that my subconscious, at the ordination, had "concluded": "Now, finally, the door to marriage has closed, now there is no longer any rescue for my desire to have feelings for the other half of humankind, which is, however, part of my nature." As a result, the subconscious simply quit service. It "avenged" itself with so called "tonic immobility", the reflex to feign death, as animals do when threatened with extreme danger, because I had given it so little attention and had suppressed it time and time again, if it wanted to come to the surface. For a short moment, I had earlier "known" that it was the loss of the love for a woman which had made me so sad. But exactly this was what I could not admit to myself. And indeed, just two minutes later I no longer "knew" why I was crying. The pain raged in the unconscious, because it was not allowed to the surface. I had never allowed it to.

The powerless, tortured unconscious now became entangled in sophisms: "You are desperate; everyone who tries to help will necessarily have to despair, because you cannot escape from your despair". And I told myself: "Before I draw the others into despair, I would rather want to vanish into hell alone".

The abandonment in the colourless grey room, where I lived in a private home far from the church and where I now wandered back and forth, was felt so greatly that I stopped again and again at the washstand, and took the razor blade to cut open the arteries in my wrist. Only with extreme effort could I return it to the glass-plate. The window, the Rhine, the rail tracks, everything attracted me almost irresistibly.

If an employee of the hospital, where I used to get my meals at noon, had not taken me out of my room on the spot, although I did not want to at all – because how should they help me in the hospital? – I don't know where I would eventually have arrived.

They sent me to a rest home, hoping that I would recover quite by myself. The despair however remained; it grew even worse – in fact through the fact that my confessor had urged me to carry on at least celebrating the sacred Mass. Yet how should I, as a hopeless, admittedly believing, but precisely believing myself to be lost, worthily celebrate the sacred Mass? I became ensnared even more deeply in the "guilt", because, on one hand, I wanted to obey and carry on celebrating, while, on the other, however, I experienced that I was desperate and therefore a mortal sinner who piled up sin through each new celebration.

My mother found me in this condition at the rest home. "Can you never become happy again?", she asked. If it has ever given me pain to cause my mother pain, then here, where she had to see my despair. It looked desperately like me actually not being ever able to become glad again, and so I could give her no hope. What that must have meant for her actually only hit my mind later. She had, it seemed to us, done the utmost for us, in the years after the war, without our father, without his pension, in the years of the worst need alone with three children, used to better and the best days, she had always renounced everything for the good of her children, had created a warm home for us, had given us an education, had made it possible to attend school and university – and now her efforts were apparently lost. Neither was I, humanly speaking, healthy, nor had I succeeded in my profession, before I had properly begun. Three months after my ordination, she had to see the breakdown of all my physical and mental resources. They simply stood still, stopped, burnt out in an inexplicable way, which had completely shrunk from my will.

On My Own Feet Again

This was not the way for me to find help. I therefore took on the problem on my own initiative to reach a clinic. Beforehand, the episcopal authority in question had wanted to spare me just this. All attempts at out-patient treatment during the crisis had, however, achieved nothing, so I at last wanted something effective to be done with me. It lasted six weeks in the clinic, until I got rid of the compulsion to suicide. Thanks be to all those who helped me get back on my feet again!

For some time, I was allowed to recover in the nearby Odenwald forest area, then I was sent to a village in Cologne's foothills near to the Eifel. The older, ailing pastor needed help, and I should slowly become accustomed to working again. This year became a happy time with many long conversations in the evenings, seated in comfortable arm-chairs. There was as much work as I could manage. A string-quartet also formed. This is where I found a priest who spoke like a father with his "boy", and to which a cordial relationship developed. Yet, it should take another five years before the fog was totally expelled. In these years, I partly felt like an icebreaker in the Arctic, the country of the midnight sun, and partly like a deep sea diver, or a miner in an underground mine, who had to bring out the treasures of the unconsciousness and the errors of the unknown of the church back to daylight from a dark shaft and who had to shovel free from death and back to life.

Pilgrimage to Kevelaer

Towards the end of that year – in autumn 1960 – I had to accompany a pilgrimage on the procession from my village in the Erft valley to Kevelaer, the Lower-Rhineland pilgrimage site, close to where my father's family had originally been resident and where its devout used to and still do go once every year. I accompanied the pilgrims only on the last part; however, their singing and praying, coming from age-long tradition, left a strong impression on me with their trust in God and their courage to confess their faith.

I rode there myself the second and third time on my mini car. Perhaps, I thought, I could find some help here indeed and more fundamentally than through the doctors. I prayed to find help in my personal need of the not completely "mortified" sexuality and also, that the burden of the depression of the soul which continued to hinder me, might be taken from me. I didn't surmise that the solution was identical in both cases.

A few weeks after the triple pilgrimage, my prayers were answered in an odd manner, absolutely opposite to my expectations. It was in October, the month of the rosary.

It may sound strange that during my prayer I found rising in my soul the dear wish: "Oh would it be allowed to use sexuality!" So, even stranger must it sound that, as a result, I perceived a blazing sweetness in my mouth – in accordance with the psalm verse: "The words of the Lord are sacred, sweet they are like honey, like liquid from the honeycombs" (Ps 19:11) – as I had never tasted before. I had already experienced it in weaker measure, when saying the breviary, in church, of good thoughts which had come to me. What should I now do with this "sign"? Did not everything stand against interpreting as if my question had been "answered" positively? Had I not been inoculated with the doctrine that priesthood and celibacy, that is complete abstention, belong to each other like church office and the virtue of office granted by God?

Yet, my exhaustion after the ordination was caused exactly by the fact that I had come to experience that by this "virtue of office" I had in no way been automatically relieved as a priest from all sexual temptations. Many of us candidates to the priesthood had trusted this doctrine, however, it was later proven that this is not the case; and where it is actually the case, it is – as I later recognised – not the virtue of priestly office, but the additional special charisma of virginity given by God to some (according to Matt 19:11 and 1 Cor 7:7), which helps and liberates them.

Ex Orient Lux

My intellect was intact, and so I immediately drew the conclusion from what I had experienced. "If any sexual activity should be allowed to priests at all, then certainly only in the right order, which God had created for the sexual forces, that is, in marriage." Soon, I was reminded of three elements, which I had digested earlier, without suspecting the consequences.

From my seminar days, I had in memory the exegesis of a Bible verse, in which St Paul claims for himself and all apostles the right to take with them a wife, namely 1 Cor 9:5, where it reads, "Have we perhaps not the right to take a wife along with us, like the other apostles, the brothers of the Lord and Kephas?". Strangely enough, I had understood the professor this way, although in the Greek text it reads "woman" only, not "wife", and the Latin Vulgate text has "mulier". Yet, the text is open for both interpretations.

Furthermore, I remembered the statement by a Catholic priest of the Oriental Catholic Church in Lebanon, Georges Gharib, who joined us on our mission meetings: "We have something to give to the world church for the upcoming Council. The problem of celibacy has been solved for us. We can marry before ordination to the diaconate, later however, no more".

And thirdly came to my mind the humble confession of a South American Catholic deacon, who studied liturgy with us at the seminary in Cologne, and who had said, "More or less all of us get a child!". The marriage of priests, it seemed, was therefore indeed legitimate and necessary.

That was the moment in which I realised that priesthood and marriage can be lived together – in the west as in the east of the church. *Ex oriente lux!* Heaven opened perceptibly over me, for the first time in almost eight years. It became bright, I could be happy, and was filled by an immense energy, a new vigour and enthusiasm, which kept me busy for a whole week – until again a damper was put on my activity.

A Village Priest Prays For Married Priests

In my naivety and inexperience, I had thought I only needed to dwell again and again on the fact that Paul had said: "Do we perhaps not have the right to take a wife along with us, like the rest of the apostles, the brothers of the Lord and Kephas?" (1 Cor 9:5). I should learn better soon.

During the rosary prayer, which I had to preside over as the village chaplain before the exposed Sacred Sacrament, I dared declare as an introduction to the painful rosary: "Let us pray for the married priests! They are and remain priests in eternity and suffer perhaps only the fate of the unjustly condemned Christ, because they claimed a right, which the priests of the Oriental Catholic Churches have". All could agree with this intention, and so they continued to pray with me. As we came to the third row of pearls, however, "Jesus, who has been crowned for us with thorns", the following words came to mind as an introduction. "Christ, although he was a king, wandered on Earth to bear only a crown of thorns and the coat of humiliation; if cardinals, crowned with the purple, in the history of the church did without marriage, what married priests wanted to do only in marriage, they burdened real shame on themselves, while the married priests were unfairly blamed."

A terrified silence followed these words. With both hands, I held on to the pew and sent a short fervent prayer to the Lord present in the sacrament. I only resumed the prayer hesitantly. I knew that I would no longer be in this parish any more.

The next day it was already apparent what had been the reaction of the well-meaning religious sisters. Via the parish priest from the next village – the pastor of my village was on vacation – they had informed the General Vicariate of the diocese. Commissioned by him, the personnel manager, Jakob Schlafke (died 1998), appeared about noon, and argued with me for five hours. The conversation continued with the doctor in Cologne for a further three hours in the evening.

The Doctor, The Prelate And The Mental Hospital

I had packed my suitcase and booked a flight for Lima, where I wanted to visit a friend and continue on my thesis there, at the place with the most urgent lack of priests. But out of reverence for the well-meaning prelate and the doctor, I hesitated, although both would not have been able to prevent me from flying. I have bitterly regretted hesitating.

At the thought of not simply going away and flying to South America, although I had already said "That is my last word!", something choked terribly in my throat, so that I had to swallow painfully – a sign that hesitating was wrong. The door to freedom would have been open for me, if I had gone. The false retraction of this decision almost strangled me. But the fear of passing by the door of two so well disposed men and of leaving the house, also the lack of courage to really obey God rather than men, hindered me from turning my decision into action.

So, everything took its consequent course. The doctor, the prelate and the mental clinic acted according to their duties of office and in the best conscience. They thought, after the "depressive phase", now the "manic phase" must have followed. It could, seen from outside, really look like that. I knew, however, that I had been released by divine grace. Only I myself was responsible for being withheld by the doctors, because I had begun to waver. During the afternoon, I had for hours been able to present, without any other preparation than my first intuition, and untiringly, the teaching of the sacred scripture about priests marrying and celibacy, without being refuted by the far more educated men, and yet I now turned my gaze down onto the structures of the current church. And in conflict between my faith in God, the statements of the Sacred Scripture, and my experiences, on one hand, and obedience towards the church authorities, on the other, I unfortunately at last decided for human authority. But we had in fact been educated that obedience is the highest virtue for a Catholic, especially a priest. I was too much a coward to heed the word: "One must obey God rather than men" (Acts 5:29; cf. 4:18).

The First Soporific And The First Shot

First, the doctor gave me a soporific. "The eight-hour conversation has been extremely stressful," he said, and now I needed sleep. My will was weakened, I no longer saw my own arguments for the existing health and gave myself up to the doctor, to do him a pleasure and show him that I am ready to subordinate myself. I also believed a sleeping pill could do me no harm. A big mistake! It was the first step to a defeat that did not heal me, but *made me sick*, because there was nothing to be healed at all. Just the opposite, by taking this "therapy", I allowed the remedy I had just found to be taken out of my hands!

The diagnosis of "endogenous" mania was made, but it was wrong, because my euphoria had an evident "exogenous" reason: my joy at the internal liberation from the law on celibacy. This joy was not "cyclical", and that, in itself, should have struck the doctors. The reason for my behaviour had to be something else: the typical ecclesiogenic neurosis had finally been dissolved. That was clear to me at the time.

The sleeping pill kept me in bed until midday of the following day, so strongly had the well-meant medicine worked. Still, I then undertook a weak attempt to liberate myself again – but it didn't help, and I was transported to the mental hospital for the second time, this time against my will. On the way, I said, still completely in possession of my resources and as on the previous day quietly and decided: "My opinion of the previous events is that if a priest behaves like a normal human being, he is considered to be crazy".

It was obvious to the hospital's senior consultant – and had to be according to the circumstances – that the man he had treated for depression in the previous year is now passing through a manic phase in which he must help him, even against his will. I had been prepared to come for an *examination*, because I thought I owed that to my superiors. My health, I hoped, would be proven soon. The next morning, however, a sister stood by my bed with a first injection. My calls for a doctor, my refusal helped nothing, besides I was also weakened in my determination through the recently administered "sleeping pills". The sister did not yield or recede, until I offered her the broader cheeks for the puncture. Whether a doctor can act against the patient's will like that today? Certainly not.

The Trip To South America

The cure lasted two weeks. It provided me with no help and only did me harm, because, in fact, I had just become healthy again. My outer appearance was disfigured to the point of unrecognisable. I sat crooked in my bed, the tongue paralysed to stammering. An indication of the fact that the medication was completely wrong. If my courageous brother had not vigorously supported me vis-à-vis the doctors, and had not stopped the shots immediately, something worse would perhaps have happened to me.

Over the months and years I could not overcome the shock caused by this treatment. An abnormal desire for sleep was the least to paralyse me. Much more still, it was the inability to understand how I could have got, with so much good will and such clear arguments, into such a mess. At that time I was not yet so clear as to recognise my own great culpability in this affair, namely my lack of courage.

Still, in December of the same year, 1960, I was appointed to my third position in a parish not far from Dusseldorf, near the Rhineland lime quarries. It was there that I decided to make the previously planned flight to South America come true.

In the meantime I had submitted a two page outline of my thesis against obligatory celibacy to my bishop, Cardinal Frings, and in response had heard nothing negative. I had also engaged in a first scientific exchange of correspondence, including, among others, with the canon lawyer of our great seminary, Professor Heinrich Flatten (died 1987). He had given several useful tips and necessary criticism, for which I was and am truly grateful. I had also sat down several times in the library of the Faculty of Theology in Bonn, and had verified the exegesis of 1 Cor 9:5 for the first time. Besides these scientific efforts, which were actually my main interest, the pastoral work in the parish and the catechism classes at four schools had passed sufficiently well. The climate in the hills around Dusseldorf and its surroundings, the so-called Bergisches Land, was better than in lowlands of the Rhine, and the climate in the rectory was just as brotherly as that along the River Erft had been fatherly.

So, I prepared my trip for South America. The pastor granted me a one-week special vacation. I had succeeded in convincing him of the rationality of my idea, at least so far that he gave me leave to go on this journey. My goal was to explain my thoughts to the bishop of that deacon from Paraguay, who had once said in our seminary: "More or less all of us get a child," and possibly make contacts with other South American bishops, as well, who had probably suffered from the problems of their priests more than the European shepherds had.

The rest of a fortune bequeathed from my father enabled me to finance my intent, and the goodwill of my present parish priest gave me the canonical authorisation for the journey. Yet, no sooner had I left the house, and the pastor no longer dared to take the responsibility on himself alone, and informed the staff manager of the diocese. He, in turn, immediately took the telephone receiver and tried to have me called out over the public announcement system at the airports of Cologne and Frankfurt; yet it was too late by this time, I had already left Frankfurt and sat in the plane bound for Rio de Janeiro.

"We Are Suspect In This Question..."

The bishop I had wanted to visit was somewhere on a pastoral visit in his diocese Asunción. I found him in the middle of his sheep, far from the capital, confirming children and blessing marriages. I told him about my "discovery" in the first Letter to the Corinthians. He did not, however, want to taste this food. The Holy Father, at that time Pope John XXIII, had expressly excluded the topic of celibacy from the list of topics to be addressed by the Council, he said. Yet, it was exactly this Council, recently summoned by the pope, which had provided the true incentive for my efforts.

I told the bishop of my arguments and he listened alertly. "It is very interesting what you say," he finally said, "yet in the present moment of church history, it is probably not possible to make this become real. Furthermore, we South Americans are suspect in this regard. If at all, a German or French cardinal should advocate the matter."

I need not emphasise how much inner consent could be heard from these words. "We are suspect," almost sounded like the confession of the deacon: "More or less all of us get a child".

I continued on my travels. A German-speaking auxiliary bishop, whom I visited some hundred kilometres to the west, quite blatantly replied to my train of thoughts: "I prefer five celibate priests to fifty married ones." A highlight!, and his General Vicar recommended that I should not even go to the third bishop who I had wanted to visit.

The trip back took eight hours through the night to the capital of Asunción along dusty roads in the minibus. From there, I was led in complicated detours via Uruguay to Buenos Aires, where I eventually reached the Lufthansa plane I had booked for my return flight, and so, after a week, I arrived promptly and safely in my parish, as if nothing had happened. And, indeed, nobody had been notified of this flight.

Looking Back: Poured Away Like Water

What has been portrayed so far and still follows can only be understood in depth, if the actual reasons for why I suffered so badly and was so frightened are known. It was the barrier which the law of celibacy had erected between God and me. The seminary director in Bonn had recognised this in amazingly clear terms, when he once – during one of my smaller depressions – said to me: "Do search your God!" A moving word! Only, it was directed at the wrong address. Not I could change anything about the distance between God and myself, but the management of the Church could!

The reason for this timidity on my side was an unconscious, uncontrollable feeling of fear before God, who so strongly drew me to the high vocation of a priest, on one hand, and, on the other, however, seemed to demand the renunciation of marriage and the other half of human beings, which my unconscious felt to be too difficult. I believed I was able to abstain, while the difficulty arose precisely from the fact that, in contrast to many fellows in the seminary, I was not capable of it, neither by nature nor through particular grace.

As I have said before, I actually found the explanation in the biblical revelation that only he can "grasp" it, to whom it has been given, see Matt 19:11, and that it is not at all certain from the New Testament that it is given to each and every priest or priest candidate to live or to achieve celibacy on the basis of special grace. The so-called grace of office and the grace of celibacy are not the same, and are not always given together by God. It may well occur that one is called by him to the priesthood, but not to virginity. In my experience, an illustration of this different calling was the double force to cry in the Easter night and on Christmas Day, the mourning over the renunciation of marriage happened in a layer of my soul not accessible to my will. For sure, many candidates to the priesthood and young priests experience the same conflict. That's why I am publishing my experiences for the benefit of them and of the Church! See, for confirmation, below p.133.

On the question of celibacy, I had wanted to fulfil the law, against my deeper will and therefore also against God's will. From the fact that God, "who inspires in us both the will and the accomplishment" (Phil 2:13) had, in my case, not given the accomplishment you can also read off that he had not "given" the will. God – as I felt it – pulled me and pushed me at the same time. The intellect and all the forces at my disposal were drawn to him, tried to occupy with him, and yet something would not let go the forces at my disposal, made them coagulate like sour milk in the psyche.

In the worst times, it was as described in Psalm 22: "I am poured out like water, my heart has turned to wax, melts in my bosom. Like a broken pot, my strength is dried out. The tongue sticks to my gums. On the dust of death you lay me down" (Ps 22:15-16). Very frequently, the following cry of the psalmist for help also reflected my situation: "Save me, o God, for the water has risen to my neck. I sink in muddy depths. No hold is there any more. I have come into deep water, the flood sweeps me away" (Ps 69:2-3).

A Mental Wreck

In prayers I sought to satisfy God, whom in other areas, I seemingly could not please. I didn't know at the time that it was the unfulfilled desire for the feminine which hindered me, yet I sensed a continuous feeling of inferiority compared with the brothers, who in their predominant majority seemed to be different and able to stride onward unencumbered.

With the help of the light found much later, I can explain the period of the ailment that I had to go through. We celibates by order of law, not by grace of God – we acknowledged our body from the hip upwards only. What lay beneath was not allowed to be, and therefore little by little no longer existed any more. There was no base for the soul, no "solid ground underfoot".

In a frequently recurrent dream I could "see" this mental situation quite graphically. In that dream, I experienced myself as having lifted myself with great effort and willpower and so became able to walk, or better hover, half a meter above the ground. It was an unspeakable joy for me during the dream to "realise" that I could finally perform what I had indeed emotionally tried to train during the day. The natural consequence of the distance from the "ground" was that I had become unrealistic, uncertain of myself and little by little a bundle of fears and a mental wreck, because of the excessive and bizarre efforts.

The Destructive Effect Of Certain Prayers

At the seminary, we received plentiful stimulation to engage in such "training". One only needs to imagine the effect certain prayer texts could exercise on young theologians of good will.

Every morning we said:

"In food and drink through measurement
The senses' lust make have us curbed,
So that, when late the day declines
And kindly us the night receives,
Through renunciation glad and pure
We thankful may God praise and sing".
(Carnis terat superbiam
Potus cibique parcitas,
Ut cum dies abscesserit
Noctemque sors reduxerit
Mundi per abstinentiam
Ipsi canamus gloriam)
And in the evening:
"The power of the evil dam,
So that our body may be pure".
(Hostemque nostrum comprime
Ne polluantur corpora)

The first reading of the Completorium – the night-prayer of the church – was taken from the first letter of St Peter. In the situation in which these words were written, at a time of threat through the first persecutions of Christians, these words were quite clear in meaning. "Brothers, be sober and watchful; your opponent, the devil, goes around like a yelling lion, seeking whom he engulfs," (1 Peter 5:8). What Peter meant was: steadiness of belief, to stand the test in persecution. In the church prayer, however, the same words had quite another point: here they were obviously interpreted as an admonition to stand steadfast against sexual temptations. Or what other kind of temptations could attack us at night?

Such prayers not only expressed an attitude of monks, they even went as far as to condemn the created. It was not the egoistic desire for lust which was scorned, but the created good of lust itself, as particularly the Sunday morning prayers express:

"Keep far from us the burning lust,
Not dirty be or slippery
The organism of our body,
For, if it burns, much fierier
The flame of hell will burn in us".
(Ne foeda sit vel lubrica

Compago nostri corporis
Ob cuius ignes ignius
Avernus urat acrius).

These hymns were not taken from the Scripture, but from medieval thinking. Thus, an antiphon of the breviary prayers for virgins, as well: «This is one who didn't know the matrimonial bed in crime,» - «quae nescivit torum in delicto» –, as if matrimonial mutual self-surrender were always a sin. That was actually the opinion of the Middle Ages: no begetting without venial sin! But it is no longer our present-day opinion. Matrimonial self-surrender is love from «God's Kingdom», and lust «added to this» (Matt 6:33), is a gift of the good God. It must be possible to give a sacrament without sin, as well as to receive it; St. Augustin had a different opinion.

Not «mastery of the senses» was called for in morning prayer – and that meant for a young theologian: in demand – but «world renunciation», as escapism, as a distance from the world. Not the impurity of the soul was repulsed by evening prayer, but rather the «impurity of the body», a thought which already persecuted me as a boy: then each ejaculation – every spontaneous «pollutio» – was something impure? Was the body truly impure as a result? Here, the disguised heresy of the hostility to the body, that is, of Neoplatonism, of Montanism, of Manichaeism, of Gnosticism, expressed itself in the prayers of the church. Today, it is known that St Augustin had himself been a Manichaean.

But according to the old saying «*Lex orandi lex credendi, et lex vivendi*", the rule of praying is the rule of belief and life, as well. The girls, who could offer an incentive to such a "delight", which in itself was presented as something evil, became inevitably the declared enemies of the spiritual vocation. From "help for the man" (Gen 2:18), as which she is created by God, the woman turned into a source of danger, whom you should better avoid.

The destructive effect of such prayers therefore corroded the foundation on which I could stand, not only in the world but also before God. Most of the other student and priest friends apparently had the grace of heading for a life in virginity, without damaging their souls, even without finding anything harmful to their maturing in these prayers; we non-endowed ones, but "celibates by force of law", and God knows and the world knows, I am not the only one! –, we had to fail in this endeavour, because we didn't have the grace to be "lifted" by God above our nature, and so either became sick or, objectively worse for the church, "dropped out", as they called it, were eliminated from our profession and had to marry.

Protection Instead Of Probation

The considerations I made in the retrospective on my education would however not be complete, if they didn't illustrate how this education inhibited us from loving.

Admittedly, student residences and seminaries primarily serve the reception of knowledge; yet taking care of the co-students is not the only love, which the future priest must practise, rather he later has to serve the non-priests in particular, the laymen, God's people. The point I want to make is that our education was modelled rather against the ideal of a monk than against that of a man who must hold his own in the world. Of course, the freedom we enjoyed, especially in the student residence was great, but a little more or less freedom does not suffice on its own, the spirit that rules education is decisive.

Symptomatic was above all the atmosphere, in which we felt more as in a great school, rather than being prepared to take on a great responsibility for other people. Jesus took his disciples with him; in contact with the people should they "be with him," the gospel says, and immediately adds, "and be sent out to preach the Gospel" (Mk 3:14). This means he entrusted them with tasks, even when they still had no apostolic capacities at all, or had probably not much to say: practice and rehearsing are everything!

In the meantime, a practical year as deacon in a parish had been introduced into the study regulations, something like that was lacking in our days.

The atmosphere at the university residence in Bonn and the compulsory celibacy law also marked us for the vacations and the so-called free semesters outside Bonn. The necessity of this protection however stands and falls with the celibacy law. If the church, the hierarchy of the Western Catholic Church, would not fear that one of its students might marry "under way," but would rather tolerate and promote it, if a student doesn't have the grace of virginity – as is the rule in the Catholic Eastern Rite Churches up to this very day, by the way –, then new and at the same time old biblical perspectives would emerge. Testing in the world and the family would begin at the right time, on a natural basis, under the best prerequisites of love and responsibility, as described in the first Letter to Timothy: "If a man does not know how to manage his own family, how can he take charge of God's church?" (1 Tim 3:5), and each unnatural distance to the world, not each distance at all, would be avoided from the outset.

The introduction of seminaries by the Council of Trent was meant as a remedy to the disastrous lack of formation. Today, this formation has been taken on by universities and theological colleges. The other task of the Tridentine seminary, the introduction and practice of spirituality, is now reserved unrestricted for the Great Seminary. Would it not suffice to spend two years living there? Future Catholic clerics would enter the "box" (the "Kasten", as we called the church run student residence in Bonn) much too early, and have to spend much too long there. Popes Pius XII and Paul VI never lived in a seminary!

A Sting In The Heart

Those who can roughly understand the pressures I had to suffer and can acknowledge why, in October 1960 in Kevelaer, it suddenly became clear to me that I had suffered from an ecclesiogenic neurosis, will not be surprised to find that I had so vehemently seized the lifeline that had been offered to me and had run off with such zest to immediately pass on my new cognition to the whole world, and first of all to the bishops in South America.

The real departure, however, was not taken in October 1960. It happened nine months later, in quite a different way to the first time.

What I experienced in June of the fateful year of 1961, the year when the Berlin Wall was built, must appear to an outsider as a confused knot of incoherent threads. Events rushed on and on and were peculiarly interwoven with one another. But the good thing was that this time I did not get stuck in the mess.

When I said Mass on a Sunday morning, the following happened. At the beginning of my sermon, I expressed my "thanks" for an anonymous letter which a concerned parishioner had written to the General Vicariate in Cologne, because at sometime earlier I had indicated that there might one day be married deacons. Some minutes later, the song was intoned behind me in the church nave: "Jesus, I live for you, Jesus, I die for you...". With these words, my heart was punctured with such pain that I couldn't but let my arms sink down to the altar and sighed loudly several times.

I took this incident as pointing to the future, as if something was imminent, and as an immediate consequence I became active. I decided to take my recently finished essay "Investigations on the meaning of the verse 1 Cor 9:5" to a professor in Wuerzburg, so that it might possibly appear in the July issue of the journal "Biblische Zeitschrift," edited by Professor Rudolf Schnackenburg. I explained to my pastor that I saw this day as a "kairós", so to speak as "my hour". As a result, he allowed me to go southward that Sunday noon, even with his own car, because I had not been able to find another one.

I drove to Wuerzburg, but did not find the professor at home, yet could at least drop the manuscript into his letterbox.

The following night, I again discussed "my" topic with the pastor. It was a very stimulated discussion, after which I could not sleep. To breathe some fresh air, I went out of the house and left the front door open. In deep thought, I walked around the mighty lime tree in the schoolyard behind the church. A political topic, which doesn't belong in this context, induced me to think of a trip to North America. Since I had already had such bad experience with hesitating, I decided to start immediately that same night.

A strange experience in the early morning, which strengthened me in the intent, took each doubt from me that I had to leave. Walking towards the nearby airport of Duesseldorf, in the hope that some car driver would pick me up, I had some sort of encounter with the adversary of God, difficult to describe, which made me think he was very much against what I was planning. So the opposite had to be the right thing, to follow my plans as being the will of God.

The other events after this incident are not worth mentioning in detail. What I had experienced reinforced my resolution not to allow anyone to discourage me from my intent. Only against this background is it possible to understand why I resisted my parish priest with such uncompromising will, the airfield personnel, the American consulate officials in Duesseldorf and Frankfurt, the doctors, my mother and even the Cardinal, to whom I was summoned.

The Professor Provides An Answer

While I was interviewed at the Public Health Department of the US Consulate General in Frankfurt, and actually did quite well, a pause of a day opened. This was the very day that I could go to the appointment, which Professor Rudolf Schnackenburg had offered me in writing for a meeting.

In answering my manuscript, which I had dropped into his letter box, the New Testament scholar had written: "You seem to be a busy man, who spares no time and pains for his ideas. That absolutely takes me for you. As to your interpretation of 1 Cor 9:5, I will have hardly anything to object"(!). A very remarkable article on the relevant verse had however already appeared in the biblical journal, he added – it was the one by J. B. Bauer, *Uxores circumducere* (Take along Wives, referring to the apostles). Yet if I wanted to come to him once again, he would be at my disposal.

Schnackenburg's letter had arrived on the Tuesday morning, after I had returned home from the airfield, for a lack of documents. I learned from it this morning, at least, that in the celibacy debate I was "right". For the other, more political matter, I came across an article on Savonarola. I learned from it that this Dominican monk from Florence, later burnt as a heretic, was declared mad the moment he went to meet the intruding enemy for negotiations on behalf of his king. Another reading was a small book on "Formation of Conscience". I learned from it that there can be no real conflict of interests; rather, it is necessary to discern which is the higher or more general commandment and interest, and these have to be guarded.

Strengthened today with this information, I set out a second time this Tuesday morning and so could go to the appointment with professor Schnackenburg. As it has nothing to do with the main purpose of this book, the battle for the right of priests to marry, I'll spare the reader from reading more details about the flight to North America.

Leave Of Absence And Recuperation In the Sanatorium

Because it was to be expected that after my return to Germany, the church authorities in Cologne would occupy themselves with me and my case again, I decided to meet their wishes and asked for a leave of absence.

First, I recovered in the Benedictine Abbey of Ettal, where I later had my "Investigations" printed, and then in the Black Forest. Through the intercession of a university professor in Freiburg, whom I had offered myself for the position of house chaplain, I was appointed as a hospital chaplain in a sanatorium in Bad Krozingen, a position I held for one and a half years.

Chapter 3
The Courage To Jump

In all these events, as confusing as they might appear, I nevertheless saw some providential sense. My departure, after a long period of going back and forth, had finally created my freedom for study. I could further elaborate my thesis.

In Bad Krozingen, I initially devoted some time to my proposed doctoral thesis on the Old Latin text of the Letter to the Philippians. The work thrived to reach the remarkable size of approximately eighty pages, and it took some months before I could begin with the elaboration of my thesis on the legal and biblical reasons against compulsory celibacy.

For a while, the "Visions of St Birgitta of Sweden" also kept me away from my work on the thesis. Birgitta of Sweden (1302-1373) is thought to have heard from the mouth of the Madonna that Christian priests, who had such sacred and worthy office to administer the eucharist, this precious sacrament, in no way should defile (!) themselves with the lust of carnal marriage, and a pope, who would dare to abrogate the law of celibacy, would be punished in a spiritual way, just like those whose hands, ears, nose and legs they would cut off, and would throw the torso to the dogs as grub. Of course I neither wished this on Pope John XXIII nor on myself.

Confusing Visions

These dreadful visions of the medieval Saint had, until then, been completely unknown to me. A visitor to the spa, however, had given me a book in which the *"Revelationes celestes dominae Birgittae de Swedia"*, written in the original Latin, had just been printed in a new German translation.

From this book, it was possible to assume that the visionary from Sweden, who lived in Italy in the second half of her life, was asked by archbishop Bernhard of Naples for advice in a certain matter. This man apparently held the same opinion as I did. He said that if he was pope, he would allow all clerics and priests to marry. Because he was convinced that married priests would please God more than the unmarried who "live a frivolous life", and thought that through their marriage "heavier sins could be avoided".

To be on the safe side and to gain heavenly confirmation of his opinion, Archbishop Bernhard had asked the devout Birgitta to address his problem in her prayers before God, and to tell him God's answer. Birgitta did what she had been asked for, but the answer was somewhat different from what the circumspect churchman had hoped for.

On the part of the General Vicariate in Cologne, I was relieved of my doubts with regard to the visions of Saint Birgitta. The official divine revelation had come to an end with the death of the last apostle or with the end of apostolic times, and only this official revelation offers the criteria for assessing private revelations. Just as in most recent times, the then Cardinal Joseph Ratzinger had, on occasion of the third secret of Fatima, brought to mind that a private revelation is to be understood merely as assistance for our belief, and can prove to be credible only if it refers to God's general revelation in the Scripture, in the same way I was told now that the text books on dogmatics would certainly offer information on what to think of these visions of a medieval saint. Therefore, it was clear to me that the defamation of marriage as a "defilement" could in no way come from God.

A Lecture Is Cancelled

Hence, I again began corresponding. It was as early as in 1961, when I was at the Benedictine Abbey of Ettal, that I had found consent with my leaflet "Investigations" and encouragement from the Austrian theologian, Johannes Baptist Bauer, the author of the first article on 1 Cor 9,5 in the journal Biblische Zeitschrift, to which the Professor Schnackenburg of Wuerzburg had drawn my attention. He had advised me to send the newly-printed article to various Bible journals, with the request for a review. A review of my article had meanwhile just arrived from Rome, from the magazine of the Carmelites. It was positive and covered two full pages. This encouraged me quite a bit.

Johann Baptist Bauer, who favoured the same exegesis of the verse in 1 Corinthians as I do, albeit with other arguments, had offered to travel himself instead of myself to the "Paulus-Congress", an international meeting of NT scholars held in Rome in the same year. I, myself, had been prevented from travelling by a last minute telegram from Cologne. And so Professor Bauer travelled from Graz, Austria, to Rome, with a Latin abstract of my article in the bag, and really received the *"Nihil obstat"* for the small manuscript – that is, the authorisation of the censor at the papal Bible Institute. The lecture could, therefore, have been given. At the scheduled time, however, only a single listener appeared, and on the basis of the academic rule *"Tres faciunt collegium"* –a course of lectures only comes about with a quorum of three – the lecture was abandoned.

The text should, however, have at least been published in the files on the Congress, and that would have done the same or even better service. A year later, I received a letter from the Bible Institute, telling me: "Given the ruling atmosphere in Rome at present, it will not surprise you that we could not accept your manuscript for the files of the Congress". The letter was signed: "Your Max Zerwick SJ, removed from the Cathedra of exegesis". German NT scholars, at the time, had a bad reputation due to their use of the historical critical method regarded as a "Protestant" method.

Somewhat later, on a short visit, I asked the editors of "Orientierung", a Zurich-based periodical published by Jesuits, whether the journal, which had already published some courageous articles, could accept an extract of my "Investigations on 1 Cor 9,5", meanwhile positively reviewed by the Carmelites in Rome, for publication. They promised to do that, and gave instructions on what the article should look like.

Before I left for my vacations, I sent a draft to Zurich. When I returned, I found a message; the censor had been to Zurich as well, and they must now operate very carefully for some time.

On The Way to Damascus

For my work on the thesis, all these refusals had something good in so far as I was forced to extend my arguments, to deepen and to specify them, and to express my thesis in new ways, time and time again, in order to defend it against the objections raised. So, after the vacations on the North Sea island of Juist, I was prepared in spirit and soul to begin extended scientific work that could well be managed at the nearby University of Freiburg, with all diligence desired and under utilisation of all the necessary and suitable literature.

But also in human and personal respects, I had meanwhile been equipped with much courage and had won backing by friends, so that I possessed sufficient strength to proceed to the end of the path I had undertaken, that is up to the consequences of the principles laid down by 1 Cor 9:5. And that came about as follows: I had meanwhile sufficiently verified the first of the three thoughts which had suddenly came to my mind in October 1960, at the beginning of my battle: the verse from First Corinthians on the right of the apostles to be married. And also the second report, namely that by the South American deacon on them mostly getting a child, I had found confirmed. "We are suspect in this question," the bishop had said in Paraguay. The third point, namely the right of Catholic priests from the Eastern rite churches to marry before their ordination as deacons, still lay unchecked in the drawers of my memory. A trip was again necessary, of course, in order to verify this.

I wanted to fly to Patriarch Maximos IV Saigh in Beirut, to present my thesis on the apostolic right of priests to marry according to 1 Cor 9:5 either to him or to his Curia. I hoped the Oriental bishops could be won over as advocates of this right at the announced II. Vatican Council. The right of priests to be married had been constantly valid in their area, and also presently in practice as Catholic canon law, with papal approval. At least I would bring home valuable information for my work from the visit. However, how should I finance the planned trip? The rest of my fatherly fortune, already badly treated so far, wanted to give away nothing more. A loan made it possible.

I thought the bishops would be surely with their flocks between Christ's Ascension and Pentecost. In Beirut, I first headed for Georges Gharib, the priest of the Melkite Church, with whom I had been in correspondence since the mission meeting of our student fraternity. It was he who, at the time, had told me of the Catholic married priests in the Orient, living under papal authority. I asked him for a letter of recommendation, and equipped with this went on well-known paths – we had been here in

1954 as students! – taking a taxi across Lebanon and anti-Lebanon to Damascus.

When I arrived in Damascus, the Patriarch was just departing for Beirut. His General Vicar however, Monsignor Edelby, to whom George Gharib, the priest of the Melkite church known to me, had addressed the letter of recommendation, was there. He received me for more than an hour and willingly listened to me. The result was, however, that he did not consider it opportune for the Eastern Church to occupy itself with the problems of the Western Church, being small in numbers and with plenty to do in bringing its own problems before the eyes of the Roman headquarters and to fight against the "latinisation".

He released me with the encouragement to proceed further along the path I had taken. Admittedly, he did not yet seem convinced by my arguments that the married priesthood is based on divine right, as I found in 1 Cor 9:5; yet he was interested in receiving further research material.

In Damascus, I was also granted proverbial Arabian hospitality. After lunch, a conversation in the shady atrium of the Damascus patriarchy developed with a very old, venerable auxiliary bishop about my concern. "But the church," I said, "must definitely deal with the problem of the passage in the Pauline letter!"

"Vous êtes Eglise," the bishop gave me as an answer, "commencez donc, peut-être un jour on le vous remerciera! – *You are church*, therefore take the first step, maybe one day they will thank you for that."

A Pentecost Sermon With Consequences

The sanatorium at which I served as chaplain was run by nuns – the Kreuzschwestern (Sisters of the Holy Cross) – from Hegne near Constance on the banks of the respective Lake. Here, in their house in Bad Krozingen, I began a huge battle; huge at least in comparison to the forces of the two opposing parties.

I thought for myself: If I could convince just a small cell of the Catholic Church in the Latin speaking West, I would have succeeded with the first breakthrough in the phalanx of high esteem for compulsory celibacy, still completely closed until then, and there would be hope that this small cell would have an effect on the rest of the Western Church like leaven in the dough.

The Gospel of Pentecost Monday – it was 1962 – towards the end contained a word well fit to be commented by a sermon about my growing insights from the East and the apostolic primeval times: "Who lives by the truth comes to the light, so that it may be clearly seen that his deeds are done in God" (Jn 3:21). I felt empowered by the Damascene Catholic bishops to speak in the way I had planned. It was not a long sermon. Starting from Scripture witness in Matt19:11, 1 Cor 9:5, and 1 Tim 3:2, I referred in short what I already knew about the history of celibacy, and emphatically pointed to the practice of a married priesthood in the Orient, authorised by the popes. I drew attention to the perspective of how important these passages of Holy Scripture could become for the fate of the church, above all in Latin America, and asked, if anybody was convinced, that he might pray with me that the old right of the priests again be fully acknowledged in the Western Church, too.

During the sermon it could already not remain hidden to me, how the bonnets of the good sisters sank down more and more, while the head of at least one older lady stretched ever higher.

After Mass, this lady came along and brought with her a sack of questions. Her name was Maria Deisler (died 1982 at the age of 82), who was the wife of a professor at the Technical College in Constance. From this first meeting, a continuous conversation developed for years, and a correspondence which gave me a solid hold on a believing and trusting heart. In these conversations, I sparkled in chaotic form for the first time with all that had accumulated in me over almost a decade, and what I had always been forced to hide until now. Maria Deisler performed a Socratic "midwife-service" with me: she brought forth from me the truth, the health and the firm belief in my matter.

Also among the spiritual sisters of the house, my Pentecost sermon had not been without consequences. About half a week later, I met sister superior in the garden. We mentioned my concern, and I asked her, whether the sisters did indeed pray sometimes for this intention.

"Yes, the other way round!" she said.

I needed a while to discover the sense of these words. Then, I asked sister superior to come to my room. Here, I made her grave reproaches: How could she dare resist the Holy Ghost and disregard the words of the

Scripture and the opinion of the Catholic bishops of the Orient! How could she dare pray exactly in the reverse sense as I had asked the sisters!

I don't know whether other words would have been possible for me in this situation. I went to the door and opened: "Please!" Later in the chapel I met sister superior again. Even then, our conversation became not much softer. Things went so far that I wanted to leave the sanatorium, if they wouldn't let me live with my opinion. Without mutual trust, I could not be their pastor any further. As much as I liked the sisters, I said in a second Sunday sermon that I had to leave them, if they didn't accept a matter which for me came from God.

Heinrich Spaemann (died 2001 at the age of 97), well-known spiritual writer and last year's director of our spiritual exercises, who had to do in Freiburg, appeared as a saviour in time of need. Thanks to him, in particular, I had been freed from the ban which Saint Birgitta had exercised on me with her "Visions", so that I could again take up the thesis on celibacy. Now, he helped to repair the relationship with the sisters. Through him, the tension, which had increased to breaking point, was finally solved and the old trust restored. It was thanks to the extremely understanding and truly exemplary attitude shown by sister superior, whom I had so severely called to account, that I could eventually hold my position in the sanatorium.

Spaemann, concerned by my sharp reactions, took for good that something ought still to be done for my health. He thought the "soft" method of psychoanalysis was right for me. He therefore arranged a date with a Freiburg based therapist, and I must say that the forty-six hours I could talk to him about my topic and myself, brought about some more psychic liberation. This conversation therapy reinforced the empirical certainty that the diagnosis of my difficulties already made before – the ecclesiogenic character of my mental illness, that is, conditioned by the church – was right. The celibacy law was the cause of the suppressions which had led me into depression, away from reality and towards general encapsulation.

"To Bear Witness..."

The fight against the church ruled celibacy law, and for the right of priests to marry, had long ago become my real aim in life. I primarily led this fight on a theoretical basis, in that I substantiated my thesis with arguments and formulated it in scientific form. The report on the way of my life would however be incomplete if I wanted to withhold the fact that I was prepared to take practical action, too.

I entertained the thought of getting engaged, in order to form a test case and be able to bring an action against the law, or to give witness of the apostolic right to marry precisely by marrying. I had planned to publicise this decision for the first time in a short speech I usually gave on weekday Mass before a small circle. In the night before, I was admittedly shaken by horrible fears, but in the morning the courage remained to say: "I take the matter of married priests for of such importance and so very much for my personal task, that I myself want to marry, not because I would necessarily like it, but to give witness, that the biblical right of priests to marriage really exists. Through such a marriage, I would express my conviction of the existence of a divine right to marriage, so that the church may one day deal with it."

At first, nothing at all happened after this announcement. Neither was I denounced nor did I meet, in the immediate future, particular mistrust on the part of the sisters. But also from my side nothing happened. Indeed, nobody existed far and wide with whom I could have entered such a programmatic provocative marriage – or at least engagement. But I had said what I thought, and could now think further thoroughly in silence about what I had said.

After The "Etude" The "First Symphony"

The research work for the thesis was finished within four months. It had taken from October to January to write the manuscript, and in February 1963 it was printed in an edition of a hundred copies with the donations I had received from patients of the sanatorium after the Pentecost sermon. Its title – in German, of course, was: "On Celibacy of Priests of the Latin rite". I sent the first copy to my bishop, Cologne's Cardinal Josef Frings. In the letter offering him the dedication of the work, I wrote: This is now, in a sense, my first symphony after the etude of the "Investigations", and I hoped he might find only harmony in it. The Cardinal was an enthusiastic string quartet player! He was pleased by this dedication, yet had to refuse.

I handed a second copy to Cardinal Augustin Bea, the former principal of the Bible Institute in Rome and later head of the "Secretariat for Promoting the Union of Christians," to whom I had been recommended – therefore, of course, a trip again was necessary, the first I undertook to Rome in this matter.

The then General Vicar of the Cologne Archdiocese, Josef Teusch (died 1976), called me in for a conversation lasting one and a half hours, as the manuscript with the dedication to the bishop had been forwarded to him. "This is the first attack on celibacy to have been taken seriously for a hundred years," he told me! Even if his Eminence could not accept the dedication, for understandable reasons, I had however lit some candles for the General Vicar to think about. Even though a badly justified matter, i.e. celibacy as a law, does not simply fall away with the poor justification, that is with the old historic reasons – these reasons therefore to him no longer seemed convincing and correct, he agreed – today there could be other reasons for maintaining the obligation to celibacy for Roman Catholic priests. If I could decide to present my thesis by questioning rather than condemning, he would willingly give me the "Imprimatur" – the church's print permission – for an abstract of six pages. When, however, somewhat later I wanted to take the Vicar at his word, he only remembered this event as follows: "*Never* will you get the Imprimatur!"

Consent And Refusal

The discussion of my thesis nevertheless did continue. It began to assume international dimensions. Leo Alting von Geusau, President of the Dutch Documentation Centre "doc" for questions of the Council, asked me to cooperate. They had read a copy of my manuscript – through one of those channels in which I had driven it in Rome –, now I should summarise the essence of the argument again in six pages. The publication failed, since I had not been able – thus the reason for the refusal – to arrange my thesis "sufficiently balanced" within the still prevalent mainstream of reverence for celibacy.

The University of Nijmegen, which the Dutch had recommended to me as a progressive institution, was ready to accept a thorough elaboration of the thesis as a doctoral dissertation. Yet, this might have required certain prerequisites, such as a leave of absence from my diocese, for example. The idea had to be dropped, since I was soon appointed back to a parish in Cologne.

The Editor of the Vienna "Archive of Canon Law", Willibald Ploechl, whom I had sent the manuscript as to many others, spontaneously offered to announce the work in his periodical. However, a review never appeared.

Three publishing houses successively showed interest in publishing the study. A German publisher suggested that I amend my manuscript linguistically and transform the scholarly thesis into a book for a wider audience of readers; later they asked I should break out the teeth of the thesis and suppress every hint of an interest in the abolition of the law, since at the moment there was "no inclination to a discussion within the church about optional celibacy".

An American publishing house declared that my work should be published "without further delay, because a book like this would be important after all those rather emotional works being published here at the moment." Yet, as long as no Imprimatur is given, even in Germany, the prospect of getting one in the United States would be even worse.

Another German publisher, whom I had contacted, admired my courage for the publication, thought, however, that he could not offer me his editorial services, because he would hardly receive permission by the bishop to print a work which touches such a hot iron.

I received much consent in letters from professors, doctors, even Council theologians and individual bishops. Among which, the remark by Professor Josef Schmid, who at that time was the "Nestor" of German exegesis, seems to me of special importance. I knew him personally, because during my studies in Munich I had attended his New Testament seminar. "In your exegesis of 1 Cor 9:5, you are of course quite right," he wrote. "The contrary interpretation is but apologetic violence, which absolutely contradicts the spirit of the New Testament. In Germany at least, such a sin against the Holy Ghost should no longer occur". Josef Schmid therefore thought, in view of the findings of present-day scientific exegesis, nobody could insist any longer on the traditional interpretation, as if St Paul had spoken of a housekeeper, and not, as in fact is the case, of a wife.

Nevertheless, there was nobody who would have advocated this truth before the forum of the Council, and would at the same time speak for me. If the staff manager of the archdiocese of Cologne called one of them, in order to hear confirmed what I had said, they again agreed more with the church than with me.

I had, as early as in September 1963, already sent my manuscript "On Celibacy of Priests of the Latin Rite" to all the German bishops. The reactions were numerous, friendly, but of course reserved. Some emphasised the importance of the matter, while others promised a thorough study. The secretary of Cardinal Julius Döpfner in Munich told me, the study had been submitted to the Cardinal. Shortly afterwards, the Cardinal wrote in a letter to his clergy that he had "recently given much thought to celibacy," which could later be seen at the Council.

Eduard Schick, at the time Bishop of Fulda, was the only German bishop from whom came an immediate reaction to my manuscript. He had one of his General Vicariate work out a reply on my study. In such detail, on eleven pages, nobody had so far dealt with the thesis. With great joy, therefore, I studied the critical voice, but I had the impression that it could not "destroy me to the ground". In a reply, I could specify the thesis on eleven pages and raise it again more pointedly and send it to Fulda. I received no answer to it any more.

I finally had to realise that the next session of the Council was about to begin and still I had not proceeded one step further on the way to Rome.

The Courage To Jump

At school, we once had to stand the following proof of courage: we had to perform various gymnastic exercises on the uneven parallel bars, the legs lying on the lower one, we had to prepare through see-sawing of the legs for the squat through the arms over the higher beam down to the mat. The feeling of thereby falling headlong into peril long withheld us from this jump; if one had, however, dared it the first time, trusting the support given on the mat, it already turned out to be easier the second time. Only practice makes perfect.

Daring to jump over to another person, over the barrier of natural fear, which a teenage boy in puberty has of the girl, earlier, in times of prudery and the strong integration into social and family structures was even much more difficult than today. To dare to jump over much higher barriers of a church-law, in trust on God's law, with good conscience, as I intended, needed, in my opinion, support from above; and I am convinced that this help was granted me, just like I had received it before, after invocation of the Madonna at my pilgrimage to Kevelaer, now in the sanatorium near the Black Forest.

I must emphasise that before completing the thesis, I had undertaken no serious attempt to win anybody over for my thesis or myself. It is true, I had already carefully asked old and new female friends, whether one of them would be ready for a theoretical engagement, to which I consciously wanted to tie no personal consequences, just for the sake of testing the juridical viability. But only after the new manuscript was completed, I became more courageous and took up an opportunity which presented itself.

This somewhat hazardous experience – as I must say in retrospect – had powerfully shaken me: The crucial test to connect church office and the conscious violation of church law with the best conscience cost great strength and nerves.

And that is how it all began. At the time of my activity in Bad Krozingen, I noticed how an employee of the sanatorium tried to address me time and again. Obviously, she had heard of my Pentecost sermon, and now presented herself as a partner for the planned "theoretical" marriage. A woman who was ready to get engaged with me had to possess the prerequisites in order to stand the fight for the thesis in the legal area, if and when I really started to defend my biblical right to marriage before the church forum, in order to start a test case on divine and human law.

As was my habit, I went into the chapel to pray and to win clarity in an open conversation with God on how I should act and whether my action was justified. On the basis of the clarity I won, and on the basis of that "confirmation" I received in prayer, I dared to increasingly confide in this person.

In June 1963, I was recalled to the diocese of Cologne. So, I left the sanatorium and served in a home for the aged. From there, frequent night trips by car led me to the woman I had left behind. A few weeks later, I had to give up the new position and swapped with another priest. At All Saints, I was appointed third chaplain in the largest parish of Cologne, in Klettenberg. A rare career! It was due to the personnel manager, who wished me well and hoped that I would prove efficient in the active pastoral. As such a chance, I did in fact regard the new task, too.

I did much in the parish, even if the weariness attacked me again right from the beginning. But in every free minute, the head brooded over other problems without my wanting it.

Application for Reduction To The Lay State

As I said, I am talking about the time and expectations of the Second Vatican Council. I longed for nothing more than to finally introduce in some way or other into the council discussion the thesis of the right of priests "to take along a wife", consolidated in the discussion. I favoured the idea of starting a test case in which I hoped to defend my right. And so I tortured myself and the partner, who had been so courageous in the beginning, with serious marriage proposals, but actually quite hopeless ones.

Not least I tormented my bishop, who in his patience went to the utmost and had leniency prevail even after he had threatened me with suspension from my priestly office. He could not be persuaded, however, to take a stand on my thesis, neither for nor against it. Admittedly, that was perhaps not his office. Yet the tension caused by the cardinal's silence became nearly unbearable, so that my work in the parish could not thrive any further. During the six months I spent there I had found a popularity, particularly with the sick and ill, which surprised me. But in the long run, a break seemed unavoidable, in order to find a solution to the tension.

The more I urged for marriage, the more my partner withdrew. My attempts to bring an "action on verifying the compatibility of the church legislation with the basic law of the Scripture" to the Holy See in a purely theoretical way, as is possible at the Constitutional Court in Germany, already failed in the preliminary discussions. My co-chaplain in Cologne called it "hopeless" for such a complaint to reach the responsible offices in Rome. In a similar way, Cardinal Frings had already decided in September, when I had asked him to submit a corresponding plea through the Cologne church authority: "It is hopeless for such a plea to be accepted". What should I do?

To understand the following it is good to recall how "encapsulated" I still was at that time. Neither in person nor in the matter was I near my goal, and within the Church I had become an "outsider". I had been swimming against the flow for years. I had no stand in the middle but was simply tolerated.

In the Cologne parish, where I served, the condition had been imposed on me to practice total abstinence from my thesis, as far as parish members and pastors were concerned. Well, I had been accepted in a friendly and even brotherly way into the community of priests and into the life of the whole community. I could, however, in public show only one part of my nature. I had to hide the other one, and the load I had to carry with this one, slowly but surely threatened to become too heavy. I had not yet recovered, despite all the portrayed activity. I simply lacked the necessary mental stability to withstand all this.

One route was left, one I had always hesitated to take.

In September 1963, before my transfer to Cologne, the General Vicar Josef Teusch had said: "The only thing we can do for you is for you to submit to the Holy Father a plea for dispensation from the law of celibacy". – My comment in 2010: Of course, they could have done more, given the previous judgment by the same General Vicar: "Yours is the first serious attack on celibacy for a hundred years". The refusal to ask the Vatican to check the compatibility of its legislation with the divine right of the Scripture, to which my bishop and his Vicar General would have been entitled, is tantamount to disrespecting the human rights and their duties as superiors, and is thus objectively close to a crime. – The Vicar General, however, continued in 1963: "You would then have to give up the exercise of your priesthood". At the time in September, such a thought was far from my mind. In February 1964, it came again to the surface, and my friend confirmed: "Submitting a plea for dispensation is indeed the only realistic thing to do," he said, "this is what the church can grant under the present circumstances".

With the thought of asking for dispensation from my obligation to celibacy, I immediately connected the other thought: If I *myself* submitted the petition to control the compatibility of the legislation with the divine right of the Scripture, not theoretically but practically in a case, my own case, the Holy See could probably not escape from having to address the problem and my thesis. One can take up a theoretical question or ignore it, not however a personal fate. The salvation of souls does not tolerate any delay and is the highest norm in canon law (can. 1752 CIC). With this thought in mind, the front of my defence against a plea for the so-called laicisation – the juridical reduction to the state of a layperson, without losing the quality of a priest – was softened. It finally collapsed on a certain afternoon.

The Blackest Day Of My Life

February 24, 1964, was the "*dies ater*", the dark day, in fact the blackest day of my life so far. As soon as I had arrived home, a terrible exhaustion attacked me as almost always, only much stronger this time. It made me physically and mentally depressed. The tension seemed to have increased up to unbearable levels. It was dark around me. From nowhere, prospect of quick rescue or at least improvement. My spirit didn't seem capable, now that objectively so much had already been done, of hoping for God and quietly waiting for a good exit. The soul only felt weakness and darkness.

I sat and brooded over a way out. A battle without an end still seemed to lie before me, but my strength could not suffice for it any longer. I feared it might perhaps turn out as bad as in 1959, shortly after ordination. I now knew the reason for this weakness, so it could not once again come to the utmost, but just for this reason I thought myself obliged not to let it go so far once more.

Now, the thought-machine started.

— "I seek a quick solution. But there is none".

— "Yes, there is one".

— "Which is that?".

— "A marriage would free you from your difficulties, you know that from the psychotherapist and to some extent also from your own experience".

— "Well then, a marriage. But can I expect a woman to connect with me or at least to opt for me in this hopeless situation, in which I am?"

— "Quite right! Love for another person, may she live in the Black Forest or elsewhere, will demand that you first create the prerequisites, on which to build a marriage".

I found this thought to be affectionate, altruistic, oriented towards the other, realistic, and reasonable. It may be that it was all that. But it was based on the swaying, negative foundation of self-centred thought: "I seek a quick solution". I, I, I. It was from *here* that everything had started, not as until now from the wish: "The *problem* must be brought to a solution, I want a bond between priesthood and marriage, and indeed I have the right to this on grounds of the Bible and the Eastern Church". I now only thought about myself.

"My personal problem has to be resolved in some way or the other," I told myself: "Therefore, a plea for laicisation! Then I'll at least have the *right* to marry, and that would be the first step towards a *real* marriage, which I can expect someone else to enter into with me." I pulled myself together, wrote a plea for laicisation and dropped it into the mailbox of the General Vicariate.

Now it had happened. I was on the best way to being "sifted out" from my priestly vocation; I had been caught on the "Sieve of Satan".

The "Sieve of Satan"

The Gospel of Luke reports that Jesus said to Peter, the night before he was betrayed: "Simon, Simon, Satan has asked to be allowed to sieve you as the wheat is sieved; but I have prayed for you that your faith may not fall" (Lk 22:31-32). I must think of Jesus' words again and again when I remember, how many priests have been "sifted out" from the service of God and his church through the law of celibacy! Not least for this reason had I given the title of "Sieve of Satan" to the first autobiographic records, when I began to write down my experiences in 1965.

Not only for me but for all priests, who have not received from God the grace to live a celibate life, compulsory celibacy is a "sieve of Satan" (Lk 22:31). This unfortunate law is based on an error of church leadership, for it is a disastrous error to think that the sacrament of marriage should be incompatible with the sacrament of priestly ordination. As if the sacrament of marriage which portrays heaven, could be an enemy of the sacrament of priesthood!

Marriage is a sacrament which has until now not been really loved and exploited by the Church; it was only tolerated up to the beginning of the 20th century. Could not the church declare this area sacred by again combining marriage and priesthood? Both help humans surrender themselves. And marriage is sacred in the eyes of people only if priests can live it. "*Sancta sanctis*", the holy for the holy ones, the Eastern rite churches say.

The Vatican's obstinate insistence on the law of celibacy in the final analysis also hinders all serious ecumenical efforts. For, how does the Roman Catholic Church want to remedy the division of the Church into denominations, if it cannot overcome the divisions in the Catholic Church itself? Because it is not at all true that the Roman Catholic Church only has celibate priests, married priests however have only the Oriental and Protestant churches, the Russian and Greek-orthodox Church up to the Lutherans and Anglicans; in fact there are also married priests within the Catholic Church, namely the priests of the Eastern Rite Churches united with Rome, and converted pastors.

The obligation on Catholic priests to live as celibates, in force to this very day, has, in the course of church history, caused infinite rubble; rubble which must be cleared, if the admonition is true to "clear a road for the Lord" and "clear a straight path for him" (Mk 1:3; Jes 40:3-4), as is said in the biblical call for repentance.

Chapter 4
The Difficulty Of Walking On Water

After I had dropped the plea for laicisation into the mailbox at the General Vicariate of the archdiocese of Cologne, I immediately felt a perceptible liberation. It was comparable with that I had felt after the "birth" of the thesis four years earlier. – Four months later, the dispensation from Rome arrived.

A Feeling Of Liberation

This feeling of liberation held on for the last three months I served in the parish. I constantly said to myself: "Oh yes, when you're healthy, you can endure that here. Actually, I would not need to go at all! But now I'm going to, because with my plea, I have also thought of others who experienced similar thing to what I had experienced".

I met three more young women after delivering the plea. The number of my proposals – theoretical and serious ones together – amounted, I believe, to seventeen; a number of which St Augustin on the occasion of the 153 big fish mentioned in the Gospel of John (Jn 21:11), had used witty speculations. None of them persisted more than a few weeks or maybe months with the difficult business, and in fact with the difficult situation I was in.

The next station of my life was Heidelberg. Cologne's church authority generously wanted to finance my law studies, although this was of little interest to me; I would rather have spent my time in theology. So, I suffered on the benches of the oldest and most beautiful of Germany's universities, the heart full of sorrow about the loss, the face full of shame of the fact that I now again had to hide part of my nature, this time the priesthood.

In Heidelberg And Rome

I spent the vacations at Lake Constance, to which my "midwife" Maria Deisler had invited me, the older lady with whom I had been in contact since my "Pentecost sermon" in Bad Krozingen in the sanatorium of the nuns. Physically and mentally recovered, I came back to Heidelberg for the new term, and could now also work for theology.

Twice during this time I travelled to Rome, where the discussions of the Council Fathers on maintaining or not compulsory celibacy had just started. I could see from my own experience how seriously they worried their heads over this hot topic, both in the responsible commission as well as in studies from the whole world, which were exchanged under the seal of secrecy. Now, I was no longer an outsider and loner but a comrade-in-arms. Slowly a spiritual position, which pleasantly differed from the pure opposition in which until then I had been, therefore built up in me. Nevertheless my strength was used by the long lasting efforts to make the hard "rock of Peter" flow (Matt 16:18 and Exod. 17:6).

In Rome, Father Gharib pointed to a book which all at once made my lately found cognitions appear in quite a different light. The Syrian church fathers, particularly St Ephraim, had already drawn from the equation that Christ and the Church relate to each other like husband and wife in marriage (Eph 3:23-33), exactly the same consequences I had dared to draw in my manuscript. The delivery of Christ's body on Holy Thursday night, they said, corresponds to the delivery of the body of the man in the sacrament of marriage. The Last Supper, in this sense, was the execution of marriage between Jesus Christ and his Church, which is called his "bride", his "wife" in Rev 19:7; 20:9. "This secret is great," says the Letter to the Ephesians, where the verse of Genesis 2:24 is applied to Christ and the church: He "leaves his father and clings to his wife, and the two become one flesh" (Eph 5:31-32).

So, the first to speak of marriage as a likeness of the physical self-surrender of Christ to his Church, had not been a dispensed vicar of the Latin Church in the 20th century, but rather already a theologian of the 5th century; and other Early Fathers of the East spoke just like Ephraim the

Syrian and took this text of the Letter to the Ephesians as a basis for their wedding rites.

The Western Church Neglects Tradition

I found final confirmation in Cardinal John Henry Newman's apologia. This 19th century theologian, converted from the Anglican Church to Catholicism, in his *"Apologia pro vita sua"* points to the "excellent words of St Augustin" which aim to underline the importance of the general belief of the faithful. "The well considered judgment," says the great Western Church teacher, "in which the whole church finally comes *together* and acquiesces, represents an infallible commandment and a final arbitral tribunal against those parts that rebel and apostatise."

Indeed: The church across the globe agrees on the *doctrine* on priesthood and marriage, namely that both are compatible in principle. So there is no duty for the Church to require celibacy. The Church of the West could adopt the ruling of the Eastern Church, which even today knows two lifestyles of priests: matrimonial and celibate priests. But it doesn't do so. After all, the Western Church has to be considered as a part of the Church which, since the 4th century has in *practice*, that is by the strict law of celibacy, forsaken the teaching of the Church as a whole regarding the compatibility of both sacraments of priesthood and marriage, and thus is in practice not "Catholic". This is confirmed by the sharp criticism from the East, uttered in 692 at the second Trullanian Synod – a church-meeting which owes its name to the circumstance that it took place in the "Trullos", the curved chamber of the Byzantine Emperor's Palace in Constantinople. At this synod, which convened without representatives from the Western Church, they said: "Since we have learned that in the Church of the Romans there is a tradition by way of a law that deacons and priests would have to promise to no longer cohabit with their wives, we, following the old law of apostolic practice and statute, want that the rightful marriages of the ordained men shall always be valid. They shall not be forced to promise abstinence". Characteristically, the Roman action was therefore already judged as a force at that early time. The Eastern Church with these words caused the Western Church to understand: With this regulation, you have forsaken the apostolic, original practice and statute!

The Bible, too, knows of no other tradition. In the first Letter to Timothy, which perhaps didn't come from Paul himself, but from a "school" of Paul, the prohibition on marrying is indeed seen in connection with a loss of faith. In the fourth chapter of this Letter of the New Testament, it reads: "The spirit explicitly warns that in times to come some will forsake the faith and surrender their minds to subversive spirits and to doctrines of demons, deceived by hypocritical liars, whose consciences have been permanently branded. They will *forbid marriage* and require the renunciation of certain foods, which God created so that those who have come to the faith and a knowledge of the truth, take it with thanksgiving. For, everything that God has created is good, and nothing is to be rejected, if it is accepted with thanksgiving; it is then made holy by God's word and by prayer" (1 Tim 4:1-5).

The law on celibacy *is* actually a prohibition on marrying. It is a common assessment shared by all church historians that those from whom the disdain of marriage and sexuality originated, by whom also St Augustin in person was influenced, and the other church fathers of the West in some way as well, were the Manichaeans, the Montanists, the Marcionists and the Gnosis. It was from their ideas, according to the witness of early laws, that the prohibition of *continuing* marriage after ordination at first emerged, and then the fundamental *prohibition* of marriage for all servants of the altar in the West. Admittedly other arguments were added, yet they only covered the original ones. At the time, the Church had not yet discovered the sacramental quality of marriage. Only the Middle Ages and the Council of Trent succeeded in doing that. And they should already have drawn the conclusion that two sacraments which all, as the Early Fathers say, come from the same lateral wound of the Lord, cannot mutually exclude each other.

Neither Priest Nor Husband

My endeavour had been to occupy myself with the problem of the compatibility of priesthood *and* marriage, and not only theoretically, but to connect priesthood and marriage in my life as well. Yet, I was currently neither living in priesthood *nor* in marriage. Therefore, in December 1965, after mature consideration, I applied for readmission to priestly service, in order to get back to at least one of them.

In Rome I handed my plea over at the bronze gate of the Vatican. I waited almost one year for an answer. In October 1966, I was informed that my request had been answered by Cardinal Alfredo Ottaviani in the negative sense. A certain understanding, after all, could be deduced from the information with regard to my situation. "This case, which to put it humanely, raises great pity," it reads in the decision of the Congregation for the Doctrine of Faith, dated September 14, 1966, and addressed to Cardinal Frings, "has occupied our conscience to not a low degree, because the petitioner proves to be sincere and modest; and that in his errors he is probably without moral guilt, can be read off from more than one indication."

What I with many others had detected in the Bible was therefore, in the eyes of Cardinal Ottaviani – who liked to call himself "guardian of the treasure of faith" – an error! But he saw no guilt in me. Nevertheless, because I had, in his opinion, "not full reign over my actions," I was considered less suitable to resume the priestly service; instead Cardinal Frings should recommend me to live as a "good layman", as had become possible for me since June 12, 1964, through the rescript of dispensation by the Congregation.

Activity In The Albertus-Magnus-Institute

As per January 1, 1967, I was appointed co-researcher at the Albertus-Magnus-Institute in Bonn, where I was allowed to collaborate on the new edition of the works of Albert the Great. So I had been successful at least in being again employed in the service of the church. In the late summer, I found a small apartment in the Eifel, from where I drove to work with a car meanwhile acquired.

At first my problem to connect priesthood and marriage weighed so heavily on me that I hardly managed the task to compare the text of medieval handwritings of Albert's works. My thoughts were absorbed by the carousel of the search for a way out of my cramp, the loss of reality I was absolutely conscious of, and the general tiredness, which still depressed me.

My thoughts and prayers circled around the question of how such a life should be possible at all. On the one hand, I felt clearly that I would become well through marriage, while, on the other, I was mentally prevented from striving forward, because I always wished to return to the priesthood. Quite gradually a certain pacification and stabilisation took place, so that I could achieve more.

The director of the institute, Professor Bernhard Geyer (died 1974 at the age of 94), who on occasion had noticed that I had found out the right conjecture, a textual improvement for the new edition of Albert the Great, suggested that I graduated, so that I would be better qualified for the Institute. Therefore, I had been granted a part-time leave to study for a dissertation as from summer 1968. Thus, my vocational path went uphill again. The problems still lay in the private area.

Acquaintance With Renate Schwarz

It was during this time that I met my later wife. In the furnished room in the bungalow near Bonn, where during 1966 I had already lived and waited for an answer from Rome, I had been gifted with apples from the garden and with further small attentions by the young housewife. She had noticed my tense psychic situation, and mutual trust developed, so that I began to tell her my problems, and soon, however, she also told me hers.

Renate Schwarz, born in Pomerania, had been resettled several times after the post-war expulsion from the east. Her favourite occupation would have been children's nurse, yet the formation failed because the nuns made her rather wipe the floor than learn to become a nurse. She then had to earn her money in a household and in another occupation of service, had been married for only a few years, and described to me the difficulties she had. It turned out that the young marriage was null and void from the beginning. As soon as I had recognised that, I was no longer striving to cement this marriage as I had tried before.

In 1968, the marriage between Renate and her husband, whom she had married six years earlier, was divorced. In the previous year, I had already moved to the Eifel in order to play no role in the course of things. Nevertheless, I felt a certain obligation to be helpful to the young woman after the divorce, among other things to help her with house hunting.

The familiarity between us had meanwhile become so solid that I thought of a joint household. We found an apartment, where Renate moved in with her small daughter, but I didn't manage to take up the shared residence, given the unsolved legal circumstances, and stayed in the Eifel.

The plan of a common *household* could emerge, because, on the one hand, a new plea for admission to the priesthood had been on the way to Rome since 1969, while, on the other hand, the personal proximity of a human being to which I could have trust, promised a degree of mental stability that I had never found previously. Also, this would have meant help for the half family.

Renate and I had already spent several vacations together, and in one of these vacations in the Dolomites, on January 1, 1969, we heard in the sermon by the German speaking pastor as a motto for the new year: "Faith in God and self-confidence!". On these two pillars, we built our decision the very same evening to proceed through life together in the future. We had to start with this vague form of a marriage, since Renate had indeed been divorced by state law, her marriage contracted in the church had however not yet been declared null, while at that time before re-admission to the priesthood, I would have been able to marry both in civil and sacramental law, but not someone, whose church-blessed marriage still existed by church law.

We overcame the barrier of Renate's first marriage through the long held conviction of its invalidity; the obstacles imposed on me as a priest were overcome through the hope that the celibacy obligation would soon be abrogated.

1969 passed in undisturbed harmony. In the middle of the year, we went on a "Thank-you-journey" to Rome, together with Maria Deisler from Konstanz, who played the "chaperon". Those days remained unforgettable for us all, when I lived together with the two ladies, who had taken the most trouble for my priesthood and my health. Living almost in priesthood and almost in marriage, I could show the two dearest persons the heart of the Catholic Church in Rome. I was free and elated through the joy of giving information. These days were among the most beautiful in my life.

All the more painful was the separation soon demanded of us in 1970, which became a mental ordeal for us both.

An Unsolvable Conflict

The question of how my further way through my life should be ever more urgently required a solution. It bothered my conscience and was the topic of my prayers. I wondered, what was it God wanted me to do? Was it not his will that I continue to fight for the marriage of all the concerned *priests*, not merely for the *marriage* of the two of us, without any connection to priesthood?

On the basis of the new plea for reintegration into the clergy, which I had sent to the Vatican in June 1969, I thought that the days of our almost marriage could be counted. At first, however, nothing happened.

In January 1970, we went on a skiing vacation on the Alpine pasture of Filzstein, the old vacation site of my family near Krimml in the Upper Tauern. When home again, in a night in January, I pondered all the possibilities of a shared life. A church wedding was not possible, mainly because the nullity of Renate's former marriage had not yet been received, but also because I never would have exchanged my wish to return to the priesthood against the bare possibility of a marriage. A civil marriage was not possible for the same reasons, especially since it would have placed me outside the church community. The goal of marriage for priests was still so far distant, and the obstacles – for my partner the nullity-process, for me the annulment of compulsory celibacy – seemed to be so great, that I could not believe to surmount them quickly. The last possibility that mother and child would go with me into a priest household as a housekeeper with a daughter, in a realistic judgment finally had to be dropped as well, because of the moral and psychic difficulties in our situation.

In this situation, I thought of the advice St Francis of Sales gives in his "Philothea" in the case of a hopeless love. He recommends changing the domicile. "If the circumstances allow you to remove locally, I advise you: don't hesitate long," he says. "If you come back after a longer absence, the loved person will perhaps say: Why, do you not know me any longer? I am still the same. Yet, the other one will be able to answer: Yes, but I am no longer the same".

I finally saw no other way than to say to my future wife that we had to separate. From then on, a process wearing-down started, a tearing to and fro of terrible size, because I could not stand by any decision, neither for priesthood against marriage nor for marriage against priesthood. In this trial, we finally decided to dare the common household as a test. I didn't stand that, either.

Twice, I made a retreat into a monastery, in order to loosen the ties internally and to find the strength to return to the priesthood; once on my own wishes, the other on the suggestion of the Cardinal. Meanwhile, this was no longer Cardinal Frings, who died in 1978, but his successor Cardinal Joseph Höffner (died 1987). I found no definite security. When praying, many times I received the impulse to walk like Peter on the water of priestly marriage, even if it were not yet capable of carrying, and to proceed towards Jesus (Matt 14:25), but I didn't know how.

Taking into account the many doubting and contradictory letters which during this time went to my bishop, we have to admire that he nevertheless was still open for my decision to choose priesthood. Years later, I learned that Cardinal Höffner had, already in 1969, ordered a psychological opinion by a renowned independent expert. Its key sentence was: "He was in a conflict unsolvable for him" – between priestly vocation and appeal to marriage. That corresponded to my assessment of things: Not I could solve the conflict, only the church-management could! My problems went back to the conflict between the divine appeal to priesthood and the ecclesiastical legislation on celibacy, which I was not responsible for.

Separation With Obstacles

On August 25, 1970, Cardinal Höffner in an audience revealed to me that things could go very quickly with my reintegration into the clergy, if only I could decide. I inferred from this that an answer from Rome had already arrived, in fact a positive one. So, in September I undertook the first serious attempt to flee from the relationship and to leave for Constance, where I hoped to find accommodation with Maria Deisler and her husband, my spiritual "care-parents". Here, I would find neutral ground, where to take the first steps in the regained office.

My intent failed. It already began by me making the mistake to say farewell to my mother and underway to my brother, and so saw the truth of Jesus' words that one who leaves and "sets his hand to the plough", cannot say goodbye to his housemates (Lk 9:61-62). I came as far as Constance, there however the fearful consideration attacked me: "How should I remain here, since the permission from Rome had not yet arrived? How should I move around here, if I cannot yet work as a priest? What should people think, who know me from earlier times, if I don't say Mass?"

I turned back on my heels and drove back to Bonn. The first attempt at separation had failed.

At the end of September, I tried a second time, because unbelievable bewilderments and fears tore me at night in my apartment in the Eifel. Soon, I once again found the strength to pack the most important matters, among others work material from the Institute, announced my arrival in Constance and my departure in Bonn and set off.

The ropes which tied me at "home", proved for the second time to be stronger. I only reached Offenburg near the Black Forest. I did not have the strength to drive further across the mountains. I prayed long before a Madonna statue near Gengenbach, until I thought I should return to continue my marriage contracted in conscience.

I remained in Bonn for just a few days: When I told the director of the Albertus-Magnus-Institute that I now wanted to remain here and strive for the marriage via the nullity process which had meanwhile begun, he simply threw me out of the Institute. He could no longer endure this back and forth.

In the Eifel, I drafted long letters addressed to him, to the Cardinal and to the staff manager of the diocese. While writing I looked up to the icon of Christ, a gift from the church choir of the home parish in Bonn on the occasion of the First Mass. I began to pray loudly: "Lord, you have called me to the priesthood and have let me reach the ordination. If you want me to return to the priesthood, give me the strength to set off once again, and also to arrive".

In a moment, I sensed strength enough for carrying this through. In a hurry, for the third time, I packed my belongings, the Institute material, the typewriter, spoke with nobody, called nobody, said farewell to nobody. There was only the pot with the marinated beef which Renate, my wife, wedded in conscience, had given me for lunch in the Eifel, which I intended to secretly drop by her Bonn apartment, while she worked. But for fear of possibly getting into a trap again there, I passed by and took it with me on the trip.

I held my hands clamped around the steering wheel and didn't stop at all. On the way, I prayed without interruption. Despite all these precautions I could only keep a speed of 100 km per hour. Suddenly I thought of the pot. The pot represented the last tie that held me back from priesthood. I cranked the window down and threw the pot out, together with the sour roast, into the hedge. Immediately I felt free and could increase the speed to 150 km per hour. I maintained that up to the highway exit at Offenburg.

In late afternoon, I arrived in Constance, for my spiritual relatives a total surprise. It was exactly six years after I had become "unfrocked" in Rome, on October 13, 1964.

As always, I was welcomed lovingly by the Deisler family and billeted in the visitors' room. I was glad that I needed tell nothing on that first evening. Maria Deisler, my spiritual midwife, who had done and prayed so much for my recovery and for the retrieval of my priesthood, took care of me and helped me over the next few days, in which I still felt completely suspended in the air. No priesthood under foot, the way to a wholesome marriage cut off, yet instructed of a positive answer from Rome, about which I knew nothing certain, I again felt miserable enough to die.

After Six Years Back At The altar

Soon I wrote to Cologne, I had broken all the bridges behind me and had only one fear, "that you could continue to postpone my re-admission". The routine session of the diocesan staff department took place in the afternoon of the same day that my letter had arrived in Cologne. In this letter, I had placed myself completely at the Cardinal's disposal. The Cardinal took the letter into the session and asked how the members would think that he should proceed with me. The personnel manager Schlafke, my long-time patron, who had probably recognised my problem most deeply and therefore always had furthered me, said: "We can rely on one thing, even if there should be difficulties, he is always fair". Relying on this verdict, the Cardinal allowed him to call me the same evening and to tell me that I could celebrate Mass again. The 1st of November, the feast of All-Saints, this year also the twentieth anniversary of the proclamation of the dogma of Mary's corporal assumption into heaven by Pope Pius XII in 1950, he said was a suitable day to be begin celebrating again.

Everyone will be able to imagine how much joy this telephone call from Cologne caused in me. In the evening of 31st October, I prayed the Litany of All Saints, as once before the ordination, and asked the saints above all to intercede for me that I may be granted the grace to carry through in priesthood this time and not to give up half way again. So, in the evening of All-Saints Day, I, for the first time after a six-year pause, approached the altar in the chapel of the Sisters in Haus Nazareth, a children's home in Constance.

I stayed in Constance for one year with the approval of Cologne's General Vicariate. Initially, I still spent some weeks in the apartment of my spiritual friends, then in the visitors' room of the children's home. A short skiing vacation in the Bregenzerwald gave me more strength. I was soon allowed to give school lessons in the modern secondary school and to help in the parish. Every morning, I could give the nuns some explanations on the Bible readings of the Mass, I taught religion to the childcare students in the home, while besides this, the work for the Albertus-Magnus-Edition continued.

In August, I took part in the so-called Nazareth month of the Sacerdotal Fraternity "Jesus-Caritas", a priest-union in the spirit of Charles de Foucauld, and at its closure I took my promises for two years.

Bishops' Synod In Rome And Doctoral Studies In Mainz

The Bishops' Synod, which was particularly intended to dedicate time to the problems of priests, began in Rome at end of September 1971. The admission of married men, of the so-called *viri probati* to the priesthood, among other topics, was under debate, after the Council had already re-introduced the married deacon.

I made use of the annual vacation to participate as an observer in this synod, as to where exactly the problem, which had troubled me extremely for years, was addressed. With the help of a recommendation by Cardinal Höffner, I received a press identity card for the Sala Stampa of the Vatican and could be present at the press conferences. With intense attention and a concerned heart I followed the debate and prayed for a positive result of the synod at St Peter's tomb.

At the end the Bishops' Synod, the green light was admittedly not yet given to the introduction of the *viri probati*, but as one could later learn, a tiny crack had nevertheless been opened for the married priest, since the bishops left it to the pope to admit approved married men to the priesthood, even if in special cases in mission areas only.

Since I had meanwhile prepared the continuation of my doctoral thesis in Constance, and through the intercession of Bonn's director of the Albertus-Magnus-Institute, had been accepted as a post graduate student by one of his former students, Professor Rudolf Haubst in Mainz, I wanted to be in Mainz at the beginning of the winter semester 1971/72. I therefore had to leave Rome by mid October and could not wait for the end of the debate any longer.

In Mainz, some weeks passed with house hunting, because the room I had found through a friend was too small. A parish priest from a village near Mainz, who was very helpful in looking after me, got an apartment for me in the house of his parish council's president. I lived there for the two years of my studies in Mainz. The doctoral studies proceeded without any obstacles, after I had succeeded in choosing my own theme: "Christ's descent into the realm of the dead".

Chapter 5
A Priest Marries

Problems still remained in the relationship with my Renate. Someday, I felt sufficiently strong to once again look for her. The first contact led to more frequent ones, just as frequent were the attempts at radical separation. The reason was a strange cramp in the heart which didn't leave me when waking up at night after such visits. Finally, relief came in October 1972 after I had considered long, how things could continue with her and me.

It seemed to be a acceptable approach if we again planned to share a household, in which I would be the priest and she the housekeeper without any further aspirations. A test of one year with regular visits should bring clarity into whether or not we would be able to uphold the distance necessary for such a relationship. The three months following this planning were indeed quiet ones for all involved, and they enhanced the progress. In order to make an even safer test, we went together on a skiing holiday in a rectory of a parish priest in the Bregenzerwald. I introduced myself to him as a priest and she as my housekeeper. This test, too, proceeded well. But immediately after, I experienced an odd change in our planning, during morning meditation.

New Wine In New Wineskins

One day, in January 1973, the Gospel of the Holy Mass, which I always commented with a few words in the parish church near Mainz, was taken from Mark and referred to Jesus' words about new wine which belongs in "new wineskins" (Mk 2:22). When I thought about these words, I compared them with my situation. I told myself, the new wine is the priest marriage, which you want in the deepest heart; the old skin, that is the "usual" form of a priestly household. Into such an old skin you cannot fill your relationship, you must really want marriage, the new wineskin, then everything will go well.

The old plan of a marriage before two witnesses on the basis of the apostolic right of 1 Cor 9:5 again emerged with more power than ever. Apparently, because I had found somebody who could not be driven away from me through all the hard examinations, and from whom I myself also could not separate, despite extreme efforts. Renate knew into what a battle she had been in and would be further involved, and actually wanted to fight with me side by side. Because of our strong personal love, this marriage should be made into a test case before a church court, in which I would be able to finally bring forth all my arguments from Scripture and natural law, so that they had to listen to me.

How should I put this newly emerged old plan into action? This question occupied my thoughts in the next few months in each and every free minute. I first discussed it with confessors and brothers, then with experts and canon lawyers. My usual confessor sent me to a better informed one, who held a theological doctorate and was a practical pastor at the same time. He, after long deliberation, finally said: "I am not against experiments".

A civil lawyer in Bonn acquainted with me from earlier times, refused after brief consideration, to take on my case before the courts of Cologne and Rome. My brothers in the fraternity of Charles de Foucauld – the sacerdotal fraternity I had entered –, dedicated a whole afternoon to the discussion of my concern, they came however to the conclusion that the exegetical basis of my matter, namely the verse 1 Cor 9:5, does not speak of the right to marriage, but of the right to take along a woman. The intent of Paul's statement, they said, was the maintenance of the apostles through gifts from the communities, which the apostles could claim for themselves – and their wives, as 1 Cor 9:5 says. This, however, they could actually do in accordance with a word of the Lord: "The worker is worth his wage" (Lk 10:7-8), and Paul refers to this verse in 1 Cor 9:14. For this opinion, my brothers could quote Protestant commentaries which were not suspected of being motivated by the intent to justify a certain practice of the Roman Catholic Church.

This afternoon's result understandably left me with an aching head. On a trip to visit my brother in Swabia, I found the saving idea: At least by way of inclusion, 1 Cor 9:5 indeed speaks of the right to marry for the apostle Paul and his companion Barnabas. For, if Paul, although unmarried, would not have had the right to *take* himself a wife, he would not in truth have the right, as he claims, to *take along* a wife. That the 'woman' in the verse of Paul's letter was a 'wife' is undisputed in present-day exegetical discussion. Josef Schmid's opinion, expressed in a letter of 1961 and quoted above, still resounded in my ears: "The interpretation 'housekeeper' is only apologetic violence absolutely contradicting the spirit of the New Testament". Furthermore, the seventh chapter of 1 Corinthians extensively treats the right to marriage, and so it resonates here. So, I calmed down again, but I once again laid the whole exegetic question before neutral authority, the Protestant second PhD supervisor of my dissertation, Professor Ferdinand Hahn. The conversation held with him over two afternoons led to the result that he agreed: "The question as to whether 1 Cor 9:5 affects the celibacy legislation, from the Catholic perspective, which considers the Scripture as principle of law, is justified." There was no argument as far as the question of whether the Greek word *gyné* is to be understood as wife, not woman.

Now I believed entitled to get down to some work. First of all, the prerequisites had to be procured under which such a difficult sacramental marriage could be contracted. I had just heard in a lecture on Canon law that according to a new civil law the civil wedding could *follow* the wedding in the church, because it is now only an irregularity, and no longer a punishable action, as from 1870 on. So, hardly anyone could reproach me for not having proceeded in a rational way after the "idea" of new wineskins in January 1973, and that I had not done what is humanly possible for a earnest examination of that "intuition".

This examination had taken half a year. It did, of course, not release me without serious doubts. Was I allowed to risk again my just regained priesthood, or better its exercise? Was I allowed to involve the small half family I wanted to take in, into the great confrontation I intended? Was I allowed to disappoint the Cardinal, the personnel manager, who had always supported me? Somewhat later, I went to him in person and asked him, whether I should give the Cardinal notice of my plan and ask him for permission for the experiment. Schlafke, with all goodwill, answered: "The Cardinal can only say: no".

Shortly before this conversation, on July 26, 1973, when I drove to the Rhineland for my mother's birthday, I had informed the personnel manager that my dissertation was near to completion, and had asked him to sooner or later look for a suitable position in the Bonn area, where I could establish a household. He suggested Niederholtorf, a village on the Rhine's right hand side in Bonn Beuel, which is actually a parish, presently however administered only by a subsidiary priest; he said I should have a look at it.

The place actually seemed to offer the prerequisites for the realisation of our plan. The staff manager, who knew my needs, wanted to help me personally, but did not, however, have the intent to support us in our daring business. Rather, he believed, at the latest after our second conversation, that I had given up the plan.

The Decision Carousel

Now a time of inexplicable doubts and scruples began. Hardly had I taken the first step towards realising our long tested plan by writing to the personnel manager on July 28 that I am ready to accept the position in the village near Bonn, a doubt again attacked me the following night about all I had done and decided. Was it the right approach, but did I begin too soon? Because there was no hurry! Without need, I shortened my study vacation and forced myself into action.

What then began, the parish priest in the village near Mainz correctly called a "decision carousel". He earnestly advised my future housekeeper to abandon it before it was too late. But that didn't help at all. One doesn't easily give up a relationship grown in eight years. He also begged me to let go of this uncertain – maybe justified, but for personal and other reasons doubtful – matter. But I couldn't follow him either. Every day, I came to him with another plan, but by the next day it had already been ruined through the heart attacks in the night.

So it went from August to October. Even the fourteen days vacation in September, at the place of St Klaus von der Flüe in Switzerland, could not remedy my doubts, whether to separate from my bride or to continue with the business.

From September 1 on, there was no need for me in Ober-Olm any longer, because the neighbouring parish, which was administered by my priest friend and where I had helped out every second Sunday to this date, had got a new pastor. So my priest friend cannot be blamed for the fact that his nerves had given out; he asked Cologne's personnel manager to call me back into the diocese, he even pushed it through vigorously. I started all my positions on 1st November, I had told the personnel manager someday, and to this date he had fixed my recall, leaving it an open question as to where to go.

How under these circumstances it was possible to finish the dissertation in a reasonable way, even if not written in a final copy, is a puzzle to me. It was the rational oasis on which I recovered from the wearing-down doubts. Because in Ober-Olm I finally felt like an overripe cheese, which began to stink after having passed the sell by date, I finally decided to leave the location of my studies before conclusion of studies.

The personnel manager wanted me first to move to the Bonn student residence, where the director wanted to give me a room, until a position as a subsidiary priest had been found for me. The day of departure approached, the heart would still not be quiet. There was however no escape from packing my belongings and moving to Bonn.

The last night, thanks be to God, I slept quietly and un-disturbed. Only a deep sorrow had grasped me the evening before, because I had to retreat so forcibly, and because I had lost my freedom of decision in the terrifying back and forth. I thought, if only you could ask once more for the position in Bonn-Beuel! I declined, however, to call the personnel manager. The next morning, the priest friend in Ober-Olm helped me load my possessions into a rental car, and released me with good wishes and the promise to pray for me. In the evening, I called him – in fact from the parish in Bonn-Beuel, for which I had no longer dared to ask! What had happened?

Move To Bonn-Beuel

After my departure I had made a phone call from Mainz on the way to the student residence in Bonn, where I was to move. I got the answer I should speak once more with the personnel manager; he had meanwhile found something better for me than the student residence of future theologians. On the phone I heard from the personnel manager that he had wanted to send me to nuns; these, however, in the last moment had cancelled their readiness to take me, now he didn't know, where to send me; because the director of the seminary in Bonn did not want to accept me either – "in order that he may not drive my theologians mad with his ideas", as he said. That was absolutely understandable from his point of view, and corresponded to his duty as their shepherd. And so I did not at all feel hurt.

But I now literally stood "on the road", with all my belongings and matters, and felt like Abraham, not knowing where to go. In this situation, my wish of the eve came to my mind, and I asked the personnel-manager still on the phone, "How would it be, if I really went to the village at Bonn-Beuel?"
— "Well, he said, "call the priest of the neighbouring parish". This priest had been charged with the administration of that parish, and I had been with him in August to introduce myself. If he would agree, it was right for him also, the personnel manager said. "See, whether you can cope with it there", he said, "whether you think yourself capable of it, otherwise we can see what to do".

The priest of the neighbouring parish agreed, and I was extremely happy about this unexpected turn of events. While I rolled forward along the highway towards the goal I had first wanted, then discarded, and now again intended, and a silvery moon looked down with its clear light to the frosty landscape, the priest informed one of the church-wardens, that responsible for financial affairs, and this one alarmed the altar boys, so that in the evening of 31st October at about half past eight, I was kindly welcomed by a helpful team of youngsters and introduced into the empty parsonage by the church-warden.

On November 1, with the evening Mass, I therefore indeed started a new position again. I was, however, surprised that as an answer to the greeting words of the neighbouring priest, who had wished me "a good beginning", I heard myself saying: "God bless beginning and end!", probably out of concern that it might take a good and not a bad end. Actually, at the beginning I already had the end in sight, and so it was no surprise that I stayed in the village for just one year: I moved out again on October 31st 1974.

Quadruple Burden

At first I lived alone in the rectory for one month, full of doubts as to whether I should really take mother and child in or not. During the day I was occupied with writing the final copy of my dissertation on an electric typewriter, outside the house. The parish did not see much of me. They spared me.

On December 5, the move by the "housekeeper" with her child took place. In the beginning everything went well, albeit the changeover of two people accustomed to independence into a closer community entailed some difficulties, of course.

Meanwhile, my Renate had "qualified" even more for the rectory household through various efforts – in addition to the miseries of separations and the constant back and forth. In spring 1970, her nullity process had started, which had cost great mental strength, and brought about visits with relatives, court dates and much anger. After two years, the process ended with the declaration of nullity of her first marriage. Renate, who had been brought up as Protestant, had, at the same time, tried to prepare her conversion to the Catholic Church. Since her daughter was baptised a Catholic, this was the best solution anyway, even if it lasted very long and was pursued by her understandably with some hesitance only — given my permanent oscillation between separation and further implementation of our plan.

In mid 1974, when Renate had already been in the rectory household for a long time, the conversion was finally accomplished. Not least, she had improved her professional qualifications, too, in so far as she had nearly realised her first ideal of an occupation as a nurse: She had become an old people's nurse instead of a sick children's nurse. This formation had also lasted two years. The year of acknowledgment with its eight-hour-day was not yet completed, when the additional task of managing a rectory household was laid on her shoulders.

So, it is possible to approximately realise how our nerves were in continuous tension: Renate with a fourfold-burden, the occupation, the motherly duties, the rectory household, and the new relationship with a "boss", who was at the same time a husband, which no–one, however, was allowed to know; myself as well under a quadruple burden: in the final phase of my thesis with subsequent preparation for the last exam, the Rigorosum, in a new parish, which I had to get to know, placed before my giant problem of priest marriage, which I wanted to help bring to a breakthrough in the church, and also in a new relationship with a housekeeper, who was at the same time wife, which, however, no-one was allowed to notice. Later on, the work on the edition at the Albertus-Magnus-Institute was added. It is easy to imagine that disputes occurred frequently and conversations were held all night long to cement the shattered shards together.

In fact, we were incidentally not in need of potsherds, which bring luck, as the proverb says. Renate's eleven-year-old daughter had received a budgerigar as a Christmas gift. While her mother was at work, she opened the cage and let it fly into the kitchen. As it landed safely on the kitchen wardrobe and slid further behind it, she sought to draw the wardrobe away from the wall. Through this manoeuvre, the top piece fell forward and its content smashed on the stone floor. As the mother came home, the child still lay trembling of fright on the sofa, while the bird happily sat on the curtain-pole. It has been able to repeat words since then! So, we didn't even miss the "wedding eve party", when Germans tend to smash crockery as a sign of good luck.

In any case, we proved in practice that a priest with a family can live in a parish, without any obstacles for the parishioners. Part of our plan had been realised. We had yet to prove it in law.

Preparing The Wedding

The morning of the last day of the year, the gospel of the Mass was taken from John, in fact from the prologue: "In the beginning was the Word" (Jn 1:1). In this parish, I was used to commenting on the gospel with some words, as I had always done before. When pondering this sentence, it struck me like a long sought realisation: What our marriage is lacking, is the publicly spoken word "Yes" that has to be spoken at the beginning, and then everything could develop well.

On January 1, 1969, we had just expressed to one another our firm Yes to marry each other. Only the "publicly" spoken "Yes" before two witnesses could initiate a public move, a change in the legal conscience of the church, from which we hoped it would lead to the annulment of the law on celibacy. In addition, I had always wanted to choose one of the feasts of Mary as our wedding date, because everything had begun in 1960 during the rosary-month with my prayers to her as "the Comforter of the Afflicted" in Kevelaer. And as far as that was concerned as well, the scales fell from my eyes: January 1 was the feast of the "Motherhood of Mary", therefore an absolutely apt one, because it is a "new" feast, which had replaced the "Circumcision of the Lord", being outdated by Christian baptism, and because it also marked the beginning of the New Year. Moreover, we had contracted our "natural marriage" five years ago exactly on this day.

I was so astonished by this strange juncture of several aspects for this day, that I prayed: "Lord, if the two marriage witnesses are available tomorrow, I'll believe that it is your will that we marry tomorrow". I thought of a couple we had long since informed about our wedding preparations, and that we had won to participate as witnesses. We – or rather I alone, because I still had to win my wife over for this plan – now wanted to build "the second floor" of our marriage, the sacramental marriage. It could be contracted by an emergency wedding only, that is, by declaring our will to become husband and wife before two witnesses. The prerequisite for the legitimate use of the emergency form is the physical or moral impossibility to find a priest who assists at the wedding rite, and no-one was indeed available for us.

I could indeed not hope to find someone from among my brothers, who together with us would have trusted the legal force of the biblical right 1 Cor 9:5 and would have officially assisted at the marriage; no one was authorised to do so, because in ecclesiastical law, the Code of Canon Law in can. 1072 declares each priest legally incapable of entering marriage. A priest would, therefore, not have been allowed to wed us without dispensation. The presence of a priest could have been of no use for us, but only harmful for him.

We could not expect in any priest known to us the same conviction as we had, namely that the biblical right is stronger than the church's prohibition. Besides, I could not expect anyone to bring himself into disrepute with the authority along with us, as we had anticipated. Therefore, I wanted to take responsibility for this wedding on myself completely.

Recruiting the marriage witnesses worked out more difficult than expected, however. Admittedly, they both came, yet in the crucial moment they did not want to take part. They explained, with solid conviction, that my oscillation back and forth, which they had observed over the past eight years, had made them strongly doubt whether this relationship would be of duration. Therefore, after mature consideration over recent months, they could no longer take part in good conscience as witnesses in the wedding. I had to accept that, and as for 31st December, we rested content with the outlook that the wedding could not take place.

On the first morning of the New Year 1974, I felt stimulated to dare a second and final attempt, as to whether the marriage could still come about this January 1.

I called an old friend from Berlin, who now lived nearby. He was a lawyer with whose parents I had lived during my time studying in Munich, where I had received much support. With his trained mind, and since he knew me from childhood, he immediately grasped the matter. Asked if he would dare to participate in the wedding, after consultation with his wife, he declared their disposition to be witnesses of the official exchange of our "Yes" the same evening. A load had been taken from my heart. I had not been mistaken with the meditation: the witnesses were "available".

It was also a great joy that Renate, too, agreed after some worrying, because her belief and courage were also needed.

I drafted a document with a new, purposely formulated text, because I had always taken offense to the old wedding liturgy. In this one, bride and bridegroom say: "I *take* you as my wife, I take you as my husband". According to the biblical model of Christ, who "gave himself up for his church" (Eph 5:25), they should better say: "I *give* myself unto you". Love is dedication, especially Christian love. So, the wedding text should already express that the matrimonial contract doesn't comprise an ancient heathen *taking* of the wife into possession, but the free self-*giving* of the man to the woman and of the woman to the man, as St Paul formulates: "The woman no longer has the disposal of her body, but the man, the man as well no longer has the disposal of his body, but the woman" (1 Cor 7:4). Therefore, I wrote into our wedding document: "I give me unto you as your husband" and: "I give me unto you as your wife".

"I Give Me To You As Your Husband..."

In the evening, we drove to the friendly couple. The two had laid a small festive table, prepared a bottle of champagne, and the housewife, in anticipation of my absent-mindedness, had procured the bride's bouquet of red long-stalk roses. We gave some further explanations, including that we did not want to live the marriage until the church had given its judgment on this marriage.

For reasons of safety, we all read the text of the document once more. In spite of our reading the text, my wife could not believe what she heard after so many years of waiting and doubt, when I actually pronounced the words: "I give me to you as your husband". In pondering the word "husband", she also said when it was her turn: "I give me unto you as your *husband*". A long pause followed, we all stared at her, until she noticed that she should indeed continue to behave as a man, but in marriage should take on the role of the wife, and she joined in great haste: "as your *wife*!"

The situation was rescued and the validity of the contract, at least as far as the expression of our will was concerned, was no longer called into question. Earlier, we had prayed together for God's blessing in the village church, because no church authority would give it to us. So, now it was possible to laugh about the "female husband", and with a kiss we sealed the seriously given word. The glass of champagne embellished the festive hour in the small circle, and we were both, thanks be to God, quite calm and completely sure, without fear, neither before it nor after it. In the late evening, at home I said to my wife: "Behold, it has happened, the clock is ticking!"

That Is "Old Hat"

It was agreed that we wanted to let some time pass by, before we went public with this wedding, that is, report to the forum of the church, the authorities in Cologne and Rome. There was only one person, who, besides the two marriage witnesses, had been initiated into the matter: my confessor. Before we could address the confrontations to be expected, the Rigorosum for the theological doctorate had to be passed, the marriage stabilised and the task in the parish fulfilled.

More than half a year passed. I had to study the material for the oral examination at the University of Mainz, had to manage the paperwork of the parish, preach during the Sunday masses and in school services, look around in the parish, and besides this, I was also striving to learn the domestic virtues.

After May 8, the day of the final disputation in Mainz, things turned better. The parish now sensed that it could reap more from the fact that it now had a priest of its own. Meanwhile, I had been officially appointed subsidiary priest, was therefore fully entitled to take part in the sessions of parish committees, and also tried to influence the life of the community towards ecumenism. That yielded some reprimands that were addressed to me by those who only wanted the Catholic community to be cared for.

It later had an unfavourable effect on the second battle, which I actually wanted to wage, quite unseen from the public of the parish.

May 25, 1974, was the fourth anniversary of our engagement, simultaneously my 41st birthday, and the feast of Gregory VII, the pope, who – as I had from time to time surmised – perhaps wanted to make use of my person, in order to recompense an exaggeration he had committed with his rigorous enforcement of priestly celibacy in the 11th century. I had planned for a long time to write down the theoretical basis of our wedding in order to be armed for the venture in Cologne. On this May 25th, I finally wrote it down – and let it rest another month. I was afraid to send the text, and I felt cornered, until June 21, when I finally sent the weighty letter to the personnel manager. He should first take notice of it, and then pass it on to the archbishop. So, Jakob Schlafke, who had done so much for me, was not overlooked.

Six weeks passed before I received an answer. Never in my priestly life had I felt as free from my everlasting topic, celibacy as a law, as in these six weeks. I did not waste a single thought on it, felt well in every respect, took care of the new kindergarten and its personnel with great commitment, so that the parish wardens finally gained the impression that I might, after all, be of some use for the parish.

Seen from a psychological point of view, that was the simple consequence of what I had done: I had "handed over" my problem, and so it no longer existed for me. In marriage, better said in the marriage as priest, I was as healthy as a fish in the water and viable, as they expected from me. My Saint's day, July 14th, was used by the church choir for a small celebration in the empty ground floor of the newly constructed rectory. The consecration of the new tabernacle of the church by an auxiliary bishop was prepared, and so everything passed with quite some promise, as with a "normal" priest.

One day in August, the personnel manager summoned me. I could easily guess what he had in mind: he wanted to dissuade me from the action. A marriage before two witnesses is completely "old hat"; many had done it before, he said. The Cardinal would never get involved in it. He only could respond with a suspension, that is, by forbidding me to exercise priestly functions. I should better submit a theoretical petition once more. Then, I would have done my duty, if I considered that my duty. The prelate meant me well. He returned the documents to me, the matrimonial contract, its legal basis and the accompanying letter to the Cardinal dated May 25, and hoped, in doing so, to have succeeded in getting rid of the matter.

I pondered some days over this suggestion, and because of the gratitude I felt for the prelate got into heavy conscientious doubts. How could I turn a deaf ear to his advice, whilst I now bore responsibility for a parish, for a family and for my regained priesthood, when my dissertation had not yet been printed, the Doctoral Certificate had therefore not yet been handed over, and what's more, my wife, too, was not at all in agreement with again risking what we had achieved. Maria Deisler, too, my mentor in Constance, reminded me of my duties as a priest and family father.

Despite all the objections and misgivings, the thought prevailed in me that a theoretical petition would lead to nothing. Between 1960 and 1966, I had already submitted countless such petitions to all possible authorities and had never got a satisfactory answer. So, I had formulated my present letter precisely as a request for examination of the validity of our marriage, and had laid down our willingness to draw neither consequences nor rights from the marriage, as long as it had not yet been formally recognised by the church. The church authorities would therefore incur no risk; I wanted to be obedient. I thought, at worst, we would just continue to remain a priest and a housekeeper, the parish did not need to know anything of it.

Suicidal Letters

Nevertheless, I still hesitated to send in the documents again to the personnel manager; and it was certainly due to this hesitancy that I tried to cut out a few days' vacation; in retrospect this must have been an attempt at an escape. It was with great luck that the traffic accident I had at this trip turned out rather lightly.

On September 1, I set out southwards with Renate's daughter – she was meanwhile twelve years old – in the VW beetle with the curved windscreen. We didn't get far. Behind Heidelberg, a big oil slick had spread across the highway from the centre to the right-hand side, where several cars stood across the road on the lay-by, while the traffic could until then flow freely on the left. I looked too long to ambulances on the right – and when I turned back to look at the road, I suddenly saw the boot of a Renault just two meters before me. The girl reacted as quick as lightning, turned around and embraced the back of her seat. I could only say: "Now it will happen!", and expected to break through the windscreen with my head – no, it lifted itself with my head off the frame, as by a miracle, and later lay undamaged on the roadway.

After a short unconsciousness, I assessed the situation: we had got off with a bad fright, even if my buzzing skull and a few tossed ribs gave me a lot of trouble for some days. The participants in the accident bore serious contusions, could however be released from the hospital the same night. The child at my side had remained completely uninjured. The police said we must have had truly good guardian angels; usually they would only extract corpses from such wrecks. – Renate's daughter and I returned to Bonn by train.

This experience taught me a lesson. Some time before, I had read in the prophet Jeremiah: "Do not let your spirit break, or I shall break you before their eyes" (Jer 1:17). The next day, I already sent the letters off. After I had rested a while and again become capable of action, after around fourteen days, I wrote another letter to the personnel manager and told him that I now had definitely decided to let the letters reach their final destination, the Cardinal, and added: "Under the protection of Saint Adelheid, let us proceed in peace". To understand this, it is necessary to know that the annual festival of Saint Adelheid of Vilich (died 1021) had just come to an end – a saint particularly venerated in the neighbouring parish of Pützchen, translated "small well", where she had "found" or opened this well used to heal illnesses of the eye; the prelate had done very much for the final canonisation of this saint, whose cult was confirmed in 1966. In my village, I myself had contributed a little to the veneration of Saint Adelheid.

On September 21, I spoke to the prelate on the phone. He had not yet forwarded the letters to the Cardinal. I asked him to do so, and he seemed to consent. He was aware that I wanted to do that for others, he said. The personnel manager, who knew me best, was in fact aware of the fact that no egoism was involved here.

What now follows is again deepest darkness. Immediately after the prelate had agreed to forward the suicidal letters to the Cardinal, a heavy depression attacked me, comparable only with that of 1959 immediately after my ordination, which had lasted two months. It always resulted from the external situation, which I perceived rather subconsciously: initially, because the door to marriage had finally snapped to, this time, because there seemed to be no escape from the loss of my position as a priest and from falling into "disgrace" in the eyes of the "world". Again, my sense of being pressed down was dreadful. Subconsciously, I saw the wave of disaster roll along and wanted to make myself small in a "reflex to feign death", to vanish. So it happened that I tried to flee once again into a vacation.

Driving Southward

In retrospect, I soon considered it unpardonable that I simply took to my heels with this trip into a vacation, while the letters were on the way, my wife in great tension, in addition to the daily work in the home for the aged, charged with the care of the empty parsonage and to be there for her child, moreover when the kindergarten should finally be opened after long preparations. My presence would have been necessary for each of these reasons, but I gave way to the darkness around me, and after giving the neighbouring priest and my wife some brief information had me take to the train.

I will never in my life forget the relief I felt as I sank into a hotel bed in Innsbruck late in the evening. But it was nothing other than the sleep of the prophet Jonah in the lower deck of the ship that should bring him to Tarshish (Jonah 1:5). I was awakened in a quite stern manner, when four days later I called my wife from Obergurgl in Austria, where I had recovered quickly. I got to know that the personnel manager had actually passed on the letters to the Cardinal. And he was now in Rome, she said.

In the course of the next three days my fear grew to the effect that the Cardinal might, before a preliminary examination of my case had been accomplished by the local authorities in Cologne, possibly have submitted the matter to the Vatican, which only could turn out badly, without enough preparation. Therefore, the plan arose in me to use the second week of the vacation for a trip to Rome, in order to prevent the overhasty passing on of the letters to the Vatican authorities. So, on Monday, September 30, I travelled to Rome by train.

I had the chance to meet the secretary of the Cardinal in the Campo Santo, the German pilgrims' home in the Vatican. By order of the Cardinal he could only tell me that this one had handed over the case to his General

Vicar in Cologne to deal with. I should turn to him; the Cardinal would however also address me himself.

At least I had been informed that the letters were still in Cologne and my fear had consequently been unfounded. Since the Cardinal did not want to receive me – I only saw him pass by at a distance of one meter, when I sat in the Campo Santo reading newspapers –, I returned home.

It was a satisfaction that they had not immediately suspended me after having received notice of the sacramental wedding. That could have happened, because according to canon law the marriage of a priest is subject to a serious punishment. As a matter of fact, I was allowed to celebrate Mass undisturbed all these days.

Someone Chats

In Rome I received a further inspiration, when I knelt at the tomb of St Ignatius of Loyola. I thought, when at home, I must needs say something in the village church, since my matter had now been officially submitted to the superiors and had not simply been rejected out of hand.

During the return via Brixen, where I walked in the mountains for two days, I made plans on what to say. After I had made our wedding "public" before the church authorities, I saw the matter in good course and felt obliged to inform the community somewhat better about the "action in favour of married priests", I had earlier alluded to. Originally, I had wanted to keep silent in the parish, as I had promised in my letters to the Cardinal, if only they would allow me to stay in office. On the return trip, I was, however, not aware of the contradiction. Anyway, I felt committed to speak because of the strong inspiration I had received in Rome.

So, I came back just after October 7, the feast of the rosary. My wife picked me up at the railway station, with feigned equanimity, and said she had done well. At home, however, she revealed that one of the leading altar boys had "chatted". He was the only one I had actually given a bit more of information about what kind of action I had started in Cologne, because he had furnished me with all necessary news about the parish. He, at least, should know why I could not get involved in long forecasts on the work with the parish youth. "It goes without saying that you don't tell anyone", I had emphasised. Now, he had not been able to hold his tongue anyway.

As I later learned from him, the chair of the church wardens was angry about the fact that I was not there on the important occasion when the new kindergarten was opened, and had said before the assembled kindergarten committee: "This Vogels must go away, we must get rid of him, never is he here, when he is needed!" I had to believe that the young man was annoyed at the fact that they never dared to tell me that themselves. As a result, he told them to calm down, I would soon be away anyhow, I wanted to marry my housekeeper and start some action against celibacy.

Not much fancy is needed to imagine how this news sped through the village and reduced the discretion I had applied in building the complicated legal case to nothing, but also all prospect of a discreet treatment of the case through the officials in Cologne. Maybe, I had expected too much of the young man; maybe he would never have said anything if I had not left the village for a vacation, but had remained "at my station", then occasion for anger on both sides would not have been seen. In any case, it is a tragic aspect of the affair that the plan to proceed with the whole matter behind closed doors was thwarted by an indiscretion. Of course it reached Cologne's superiors.

The Church Responds

The authorities in Cologne forbade me to speak to the community on my own matter, and even to the parish committees, who had already dealt with the issue. This didn't happen directly, but rather through the neighbouring priest, who had the unpleasant task of delivering me one piece of bad news after the other. Moreover, he, together with the parishioners, had to face the music which I had unwillingly prepared for them.

I owe my deepest respect to the pastor of the parish of Saint Adelheid in Pützchen, Hans-Ludwig Schumacher (died 1998), because he always behaved in exemplary confraternal fashion, never reproachful, which is close to a miracle, since he had been completely unaware of what I had in mind. I wanted to spare him, in contrast to the priest in Mainz, the participation in the "decision-making carousel".

In the course of the following week, the decree issued by the General Vicariate arrived saying that from the coming Sunday already I was no longer allowed to celebrate the Sunday Mass. This measure was not meant as a penalty, it said, but should serve to calm the community. I was therefore released from any task in the parish, and reflected on what to do. The personnel manager and some brothers of the sacerdotal fraternity came to see me and urged me not to talk to the newspapers. I didn't intend to anyway. The personnel manager, who was aghast that the matter had been let out – because he had always relied on my fairness –, reported that the Cardinal had ordered an opinion from the Canon lawyer in Bonn, of which he only knew that it described the suspension as unavoidable. That induced me to think of a renewed intervention, because I didn't want to give up my priesthood peacefully.

The General Vicar, to whom I should turn, had meanwhile followed the Cardinal, I was told, and now was also in Rome with important documents in his briefcase, and would be there up to the following Sunday in order to talk with the Cardinal about my case, among other things. I therefore believed I could do nothing better than once more post-haste leave for Rome to prevent the two highest hierarchies deciding on me before I had been heard, and to submit, if necessary, an immediate appeal against such a decision in Rome.

My wife by all means sought to keep my back free. You can, however, not side track a steam engine under high pressure. So I took the express train to Frankfurt, from there a plane to Rome, and in the evening of October 11, at 22.30, I arrived at the airfield Fiumicino. A German sister took me in the car which had picked her up to the Headquarters of her order, the villa Maria Regina on the Monte Mario.

Conversation In The Campo Santo

The next morning at eleven o'clock, I again knocked at the door of the Campo Santo, after one week only. The Cardinal's secretary was aghast and disapproved of my hectic activity. I said: "Did you think I would sit stock still at home like a rabbit before the snake and wait until the suspension is inflicted on me?"

The secretary replied, a suspension would not fall from heaven, the delinquent must be heard beforehand, according to canon law. I had anticipated canon 2388 of the old Codex Iuris Canonici would have automatically imposed the penalty immediately, when a priest marries. Obviously, I did not know the procedural law.

The General Vicar would have turned to me himself, if he had not had to travel to Rome, the secretary said. Now, he would probably have no time for me, because he would already be leaving this Saturday afternoon, and, moreover, had just left the house. He said he regarded the personnel manager's interpretation of the canon lawyer's opinion from Bonn, namely that a suspension is unavoidable, at least as a very much simplified interpretation.

Despite the unhappy time at which I came, the secretary nevertheless got the General Vicar by telephone in the Collegium Germanicum, where he and the Cardinal had been invited for dinner, and arranged a conversation with me for the early afternoon.

General Vicar Peter Nettekoven (died 23.4.1975) had earlier been diocesan youth pastor and had remained a pastor in his office in the diocese administration, as well. So, he felt the burden of his task, which put him time and time again to the crucial test between caring for people, on the one hand, and canon law, on the other. The conversation between the two of us also proved painful for him, because he had hoped we could find an agreement, while I wanted to remain hard for the sake of the matter.

Three hours were left to prepare for the conversation. I spent it for the most part in front of St Peter's tomb in St Peter's Cathedral, and then ate a minestrone soup.

The conversation began at half past two in the afternoon and lasted three quarters of an hour. The General Vicar began with the question of what he should think of the toing and froing. At first they had applied for dispensation, so that I could marry, and then I had not wanted that. As a consequence, the Cardinal in person had interceded for me so that I was re-admitted into the priestly service. Hardly am I back in the service, and this wouldn't do either. I had made a contract, which I had signed together with two persons as witnesses, a paper that should best be torn to pieces, since it was "a nullum", null and void, according to ecclesiastical law.

"What do you actually want?", asked the General Vicar.

I asked him whether he had not read my letters to the Cardinal. Yes, he had read them, he replied. I explained that I could neither live in the priesthood alone nor in marriage alone, but that I eventually had arrived at the conclusion that I have the calling to priesthood and marriage.

"Before your ordination, you completely voluntarily and after mature consideration accepted the condition required by the Latin Church to remain celibate, and you even asked for ordination," the General Vicar replied, this follows from the records".

"If we had known before ordination that it is possible in the Catholic Eastern rite Churches to marry before ordination, many of us would have taken a different decision," I replied. "In so far as the church had told us nothing about this, maybe it has some redressing to do for some of us".

"I, for my part, knew before ordination, and I assume you knew that, too", Nettekoven replied. — "I didn't", I said, "I only learned this from a member of the Eastern Rite Church".

"In any case, the Latin Church only accepts those as candidates for the priesthood who renounce the right to marriage," he emphasised. And I returned: "Then this Church is just *Latin*, not *Catholic*!"

Without agreeing, General Vicar Nettekoven specified: "The church accepts those who have the *charisma* of celibacy. Our Cardinal tells all the students of theology this". "No, I replied, "this is what the Church has only said since the Second Vatican Council. Before this, they only spoke of an *obligation* of the clergy to celibacy!"

I continued. The Second Vatican Council has, for the first time, underlined the fact that celibacy is a special charisma, which is not given to all. It did so on the basis of an intervention by Cardinal Döpfner, which partially originated from my texts. Whereupon the Council extricated itself, regarding the law, by answering that one should pray for this charisma, as expressly said in article 16 of the "Presbyterorum Ordinis", the decree on Service and Life of Priests.

Besides, the Latin Church with its condition of compulsory celibacy is at variance with the Holy Scripture – something the General Vicar immediately vigorously denied –, because in the Pastoral Letters St Paul or his disciple says, the priest shall be "the husband of one wife" (1 Tim 3:2), therefore he *can* be husband of a wife; the Latin Church, however says, he could *not* be a wife's husband.

"Do you admit that this is a contradiction?", I asked. Not like this!", he replied. "What does 'not like this mean?'", I asked back. *Somehow*, Nettekoven admitted a contradiction, I think.

The Cardinal's Decision

Consequently, the General Vicar went on to clarify, if not the general problem, at least my personal case. "Try to live as a Christian," he said. "The Cardinal will allow you – by contrast to what is usually done – to continue your work in the Albertus-Magnus-Institute, so that you can earn your living and find possible fulfilment for your life in scientific work. That is also a service for the church, as others have rendered. And if you want to marry, provide the prerequisites, as the scientists and priests Stephan Pfürtner, Diego Arenhövel and Otto Hermann Pesch have done in recent times".

"You simply let the best people go, and their priesthood for you is not worth as much?", at which I snapped with the fingers.

Nettekoven then announced the Cardinal's decision. "I can tell you so much that the Cardinal prohibits you from exercising priestly activities. Live as Christian and provide the prerequisites for a marriage, but do not try to upset the order of the Latin Church. That is wrong!"

"From where do you know that? From where do you know that!" I asked him and stared at him with the same firmness as he at me.

"Because marriage is impossible after ordination, even in the Oriental Church. The entire Church agrees on that".

I said I was aware that this would be a great difficulty. I could appeal against it only on the statement of St Paul: "Do we perhaps not have the right to take along a sister as a wife, like the other apostles and Peter?" (1 Cor 9:5).

The General Vicar surmised that Paul had said this in those days, but we are now in the year 1974. On the whole, he found nearly nothing new in my letter. I said: "So far, no-one has appealed to 1 Cor 9:5, and that is an apostolic right of the highest authority. The church law, however, against which I am fighting, is only 835 years old. It dates from 1139, when the Second Lateran Council pronounced the nullity of the marriage of a cleric."

Nettekoven then spoke of the possibility of losing the charisma. He didn't want to say that this was the situation in my concrete case; the last judgment on my life rests with God, not with him, he said.

I said I was convinced by what I had suffered and meditated, to have been commissioned to give witness of the *double* calling by God to priesthood and marriage, because obviously I had not received the charisma needed for celibacy, despite intense prayer. I wanted to fight for the right of priests to marry, and had thereby in mind to help the many priests who have gone from the frock with the goal of marriage, which is, in fact, a major loss for the Church.

"It is true", the General Vicar replied, "some have gone...".

I further reminded him of the legal dissimilarity in the Catholic Church between East and West. "Imagine in Germany, for example, marriage being allowed in Bavaria, but prohibited in North Rhine-Westphalia. Does God make the calling to priesthood and marriage only rain down regionally, in the Orient, but not in the West?"

The General Vicar replied, civil rights were something quite different, and the Latin Church simply takes its priests only from those who have the charisma.

"With what kind of justification does it then complain of a shortage of priests?", I returned.

"That is another question. I just want to advise you to keep away from the general problem. You will ruin yourself in doing so".

"Jesus, too, ruined himself, so did Paul, but that doesn't matter", I said. "If only the problem of rights is promoted! I trust in God, not in me."

"That is what we all do", the General Vicar replied, "trust that he will lead us."

"Then we can agree on that", I said.

Eventually, we did indeed turn to my personal case. The General Vicar repeated that from now on I was prohibited from exercising any priestly activities or duties. I asked, whether that was the "*suspensio a divinis*".

"No, the General Vicar replied, "because the *suspensio a divinis* is a penalty. This cannot be inflicted without guilt, and that is not given in your case."

"Then why the prohibition?"

"That is what I just explained to you, because you don't acknowledge the priesthood of the Latin Church. Because you signed this paper, which is a nullum in our eyes. You wrote in your letter that you have not lived this marriage, and I trust you, but through the presentation of this document you showed that you do not approve of the celibate priesthood. The contract itself is invalid."

"And you simply sweep my appeal on divine right from the table?".

"No, I do not do that at all," said the General Vicar, thinking perhaps of the fact that they did not charge me with an offence, but suggested once more, that I should provide the prerequisites for a marriage.

"You mean, I should ask once more for reduction to the lay state? I have already done this, but that doesn't help me, because priesthood alone and marriage alone are unbearable for me."

"You cannot say that. The work at the Albertus-Magnus-Institute is also a fulfilling activity. You give thereby witness as a Christian".

"Yet I am a priest," I said. Then, I thanked him for the opportunity to continue working at the Institute. However, my last word was: "I shall appeal in Rome against the prohibition".

Outside the door, the General Vicar confirmed that he would hand me the prohibition in writing. Because without it, I could not appeal against it.

"The Latin Church Doesn't Love The Prophets..."

Somewhat later, I visited the priest of the Melkite Church, who had made me aware of the married priests in the Catholic Churches of the Orient and who still worked in Rome, Georges Gharib. In the conversation with him, I sought to arrange my thoughts and wrote down some notes about my conversation in the Campo Santo. Jesus' saying was quoted: "It is unthinkable that a prophet dies outside Jerusalem" (Lk 13:33). "L'église Latine n'aime pas les prophètes", he said: "The Latin Church does not love the prophets."

On the following days, I took advantage of being in Rome to catch up with the necessary information on where to lodge the appeal against the prohibition of priestly activities, which should not be a suspension. A friend in the Sant' Uffizio finally referred me to a Hungarian Monsignor in the Congregation for the Clergy, who spoke German and was probably competent also.

I first talked quite theoretically with this Monsignor about what could be done, if the bishop forbids the celebration of Mass, but pronounces no suspension. He said, this might have political reasons, as happened in England and Ireland, or other reasons.

"In any case, there is a remedy: Appeal to the Holy See", the Monsignor said. "We will hear the bishop and then adjudicate *secundum aequum et bonum et iustum*", that is: in accordance with what is appropriate, good and just.

The Community Is Informed

At home, the waves had meanwhile nothing less than smoothed. In the last fourteen days of October, Renate and I lived in the parsonage completely cut off from the environment. No telephone calls, no visits, nobody broke through the isolation. Just that they didn't smash our windows! The mood outdoors was like that, as somebody later reported. Marriage of a priest at that time was still regarded as something absolutely monstrous.

I also kept myself back and saw nobody, as long as nobody wanted to know anything. I was waiting for written confirmation by the General Vicar of my the prohibition to exercise my office.

The letter from Cologne only arrived on October 26, a Saturday morning, per express letter. I am forbidden from all priestly activity, it said. My attempted marriage was, *objectively*, an act threatened with excommunication. I should move out from the parsonage. I could continue the work at the Institute. If I wanted to marry, I should submit a renewed plea for dispensation.

On the next day, Sunday, October 27, was therefore the last day to say something in the parish, because I still lived there and nothing had been officially decided on the future character of my priesthood. I wanted to use this final opportunity to address some words, just three sentences, to the community, and that in the evening Mass already, after the proclamations, which the retired secondary school teacher would read at the beginning.

The evening came, I went into the sacristy. The pastor of St Adelheid, who was also officially responsible as the pastor for this village, had come himself to read the proclamations. Part of it was a letter from Cologne; I could easily surmise its content. Since he was already in the church to read the text, I could not speak to him.

The letter ran: "Hereby, Rector Vogels is released from his duties as a subsidiary priest at St Antonius. He retains his activities at the Albertus-Magnus-Institute of the diocese."

As the pastor was about to leave the pulpit to go into the confessional, I stepped to him and quietly asked, whether I could also say a few words also. He allowed it.

I turned to the community and said: "Please listen to me for a moment. I *ask* you for that favour, otherwise I would have to shake the dust from my feet, as the Lord says (see Matt 10:14). I only want to say three sentences. Is it not true, including for you, that marriage is something holy? – Isn't marriage a sacrament for you, too? Do you not all, who live in the sacrament of marriage, approach the altar and take the Body of Christ into your hands? Thank you for your attention."

I went. With these words, I had only proclaimed the common belief and said nothing about my person, except indirectly by saying "also for you". I wanted to stimulate reflection on the deeper problem of the alleged incompatibility of the two sacraments of priesthood and marriage. In retrospect, I knew now, why I had to prepare this public statement against my original intention, at the instigation received during my prayers in St Ignatius in Rome.

A Nightly Parish Council Session

Up to the next morning, everything remained quiet. In the high Mass on the day, I tried to say the same again, anticipated, however, that I might be prevented from doing so. Actually, Adelheid's pastor and three members of the parish executive, the Church Executive, stood in the sacristy determined to hold me back. So, in rough lines, I explained my behaviour to at least the three men of the church executive. A minimum of understanding seemingly opened up in their minds.

In the course of the next few days, I paid several visits to parish-members, who – as I heard and could myself imagine – were, in particular, concerned about the events, because I had served them as priest. Among others, I saw the chair of the parish executive in order to give him the opportunity to assess the events. Here, too, I found understanding, even benevolence.

On October 29, about 10 o'clock in the evening, I got a phone call. A joint session of the parish council and the church executive was being held, and I should come as well. Although I was somewhat doubtful about the purpose of the invitation, I was happy to make myself understood to a wider audience.

The mood there was, however, quite different. I asked the chairman of the parish executive, whether he had reported that I acted on behalf of a general problem and that I wanted to remain a priest. He confirmed this. As it turned out, however, the intent of the two combined parish committees was to demand from me that I should stop visiting parish members, because they "disturbed the peace". In consequence, I asked the three I had visited to present, in turn: "Did you feel disturbed by my visit?". All three answered: "No!".

"How can you then claim that my visits disturb the peace?" I asked the chair of the parish council. He kept silent. When, moreover, the chair of the parish executive, who yesterday had wished me good luck for my business, agreed with him: "In any case the visits must stop!", I got up and left the room, in order to say at home: "We're moving out on November 1."

Actually, we succeeded from one day to the next to get a furniture remover October 31, and so I left the parish exactly one year after I had come.

Escape Into A Convent

Except for the few parish members who could be counted on one hand, nobody said goodbye, they simply let me go just as quickly and inconspicuously as I had come, in the night. I was not yet allowed to come to daylight with my findings.

We had tried to put the new wine of a priest marriage into the old wineskin of a priest household (cf. Lk 5:37): the wine had burst the skin and the wine was about to be spilt. The day before our departure, my good wife almost alone had to pack all the suitcases and parcels with my books - it was the third move in one year –, because I had to formulate an answer to the written prohibition on me exercising priestly functions. The response deadline ran out on November 1. I could not give myself up and did not yield to the demand to disavow my marriage contract. The letter went out from my new apartment to the Holy See at the same time as my written appeal, namely on November 1. I only received an answer from Rome on March 25, 1976: an anonymous expert opinion. But the matter had meanwhile been settled in Cologne.

I could stand living in a private apartment in Bonn Beuel for a month. Deprived of the possibility of public celebration, I felt I had been pushed off-side, so it seemed to me that this could only be a dead end. Was I not sitting before a pile of shards? After four years of renewed priesthood, everything I had built up was back in ruins!

So much was certain for me: I wanted, by all means to remain in the priesthood, because only from there could I fulfil the task I felt commissioned to by God. Because it belonged to my life-task to connect priesthood and marriage, my conscience did not keep silent: I could not give up the priesthood. During the night, I had to endure terrible fears of a kind that an outsider can hardly imagine. I only saw one way out: Get out of the house, get out of the marriage, get out from the world – into a convent.

Finally, on December 5, I succeeded in escaping to the train to Siegburg with a suitcase, and from there to Hachenburg in the Westerwald, where I had asked the Cistercian friars of Marienstatt, if I could come as a guest for a while. I told the abbot quite frankly, I am a priest who wants to separate from a woman. On December 6, I sent a letter of subjection limited by provisos to Cologne's General Vicar.

Conversation In Marienstatt

In the first few days, being torn between the sacrament of priesthood and that of marriage made itself noticed like being physically torn to pieces, so that I wrote a heart-wrenching letter to the Cardinal. I asked him to help me, for the sake of Christ's love and as my bishop: "This is not my problem, but the problem of the Church".

On the next weekend, the Cardinal actually sent a prelate to Marienstatt, namely the former director of the Bonn seminary, Hans Daniels, now acting General Vicar, in order to offer me a small position as a priest in a rest home, on grounds of my subjection. He died in 1992 at the age of 86.

I stayed another week in Marienstatt. I had taken material from the Institute with me and was, therefore, not unoccupied. On the following Saturday, the acting General Vicar once again came to the abbey and specified his idea of my future service. I asked him, why they had actually not pronounced the suspension as a penalty but only a prohibition to exercise priestly functions, which, in my opinion, is not at all possible in canon law.

For, on the dubiety of this prohibition, which had expressly not been issued as a penalty, I had based my appeal against the prohibition to the Holy See, and saw the lack of a suspension as a first victory of my argument with the divine right: If the penalty which normally follows an attempt at marriage had not come down on me, then they had at least recognised that I was acting in good faith, and consequently they had seen no possibility to punish me, because no guilt was given. Then, I was the first to violate the law of celibacy unpunished; my belief in the divine right of 1 Cor 9:5 had already won.

The acting General Vicar poured a good dash of water into this wine, telling me that I was actually "irregular", that is incapable of exercising priestly functions, because of the former "illness", and it would therefore depend on the discretion of the bishop as to how far he allows me to practise priestly functions. The irregularity is no penalty, but a consequence of the illness. My arguments had not been considered in the course of imposing the prohibition and avoiding the suspension.

I replied that General Vicar Nettekoven had, neither in the conversation I had with him in Rome, nor in his letter dated October 24, alluded to anything of this kind. I got the answer he, the acting General Vicar, had drafted this letter, and he had in mind the irregularity on the grounds of the "illness", when he said that the "attempted marriage" was *objectively*, even if not subjectively, a crime punishable by excommunication.

I could deduce how healthy he took me for from the fact that he told me he took me for ill. You cannot bluntly tell a truly mentally ill person that he is sick. In so saying, he induced my total resistance.

I conceded that earlier there had been a kind of illness, which however originated precisely from the law of celibacy and was only a temporary neurosis. My continuing improvement, since I had realised the reason for the depression through prayers in Kevelaer, was clear proof of this diagnosis being right.

"Let it rest", the acting General Vicar answered. Anyway, he could say nothing against it. He left me with the concrete offer, namely that I should have a look at the rest-home in Siegburg.

Departure Is Difficult

While still in Marienstatt, amidst prayers, I found it necessary to carry out the originally planned winter vacation with my wife. She sorely needed this relaxation after the month long strain. From there, however, I wanted to continue the journey to Rome, in order to forestall a possible message from the acting General Vicar of the kind: "The man is sick". For, if the Roman authorities got to hear nothing else from Cologne, my appeal to the Holy See and my whole endeavour to make the Roman Curia deal with the respective theoretical question was, from the outset, condemned to failure. That had to be prevented by all means.

Therefore, it seemed to me that I had to leave the convent, and about this question I talked in detail with my adviser in the abbey. He agreed. Nevertheless, my parting from Marienstatt turned out to be difficult. Twice, I postponed my departure and revoked it, so that the abbot and the host-father could only silently shake their head. I could not suppress the doubt that the decision to leave the monastic peace that made me breathe in the depth of my soul and feel at home as in the Berlin Heart of Jesus Church, was only a temptation, since I had wanted to stay here for as long as possible. That a position had been offered to me in Cologne; that the confessor had agreed that I must go to the Vatican; that the thought was born from prayer – I had forgotten everything. I almost could not break away. When, after a final hesitation, I wanted to pray before the tabernacle, I noticed that I couldn't. Heaven seemed locked. Without saying a word, I got up, packed my suitcase and had me taken to the railway station. It was December 24, 1974.

Chapter 6
The Wearing Down Feud

During his visit to Marienstatt before Christmas 1974, the acting General Vicar had suggested looking at a rest-home in Siegburg, where I could get the position of a curate, so far held by a Benedictine monk of the nearby Siegburg Abbey. But the abbot pointed to another small community the Siegburg Fathers served, namely the hospital in Porz-Wahn near the airport. Getting there was much further for the monks than to the nearby rest-home. So I agreed to take over celebrating Mass there.

During the next four years, I could celebrate the daily Mass with the "Poor Maids of Jesus Christ" in St. Josef's hospital in Wahn and probably received just as much as I could give.

Even if I felt quite well in my lodging in Wahn, I had no space to put my books and also found no opportunity to become integrated into the parish work in Wahn, because another chaplain was there. After becoming more courageous, I moved back into my apartment in Beuel to my family, to Renate and her daughter, in August 1975. The General Vicariate tacitly tolerated it, after I had communicated the move.

The Doctorate

My work at the Albertus-Magnus-Institute proceeded fairly well. I had been entrusted with reviewing the fourth book of Albert's commentary on the Sentences of Petrus Lombardi on the sacraments. I had furthermore to collaborate on the edition of the first volume of his Summa Theologiae and proof-read all the other volumes prepared. Above all, I finally succeeded in preparing the printing of my dissertation "Christ's Descent into the Realm of the Dead". By the mediation of Professor Karl Lehmann from Freiburg, later to become bishop of Mainz and a Cardinal, whom I had met before the house in conversation with a brother from my sacerdotal fraternity, it was accepted into the "Freiburger Theologische Studien". Their then editor, professor Riedlinger, wrote to me on March 18, 1975: "Your work is convincing, stimulating, ecumenically exemplary." In May of the same year, I was able to sign the contract with the publishing house Herder in Freiburg, and so had complied with all requirements for the doctorate.

On May 28, 1975, I had to profess the Tridentine Creed before the Dean of the Catholic theological faculty in Mainz, and then the diploma was handed over, and I was allowed to use the title of Dr.

The printing of my dissertation, supported by the diocese of Cologne, took more than one year. Yet on May 31, 1976, I held the first twenty copies in my hands, offered by the publisher, and equipped with these undertook a short trip to friends and sponsors of the work, dared even to visit Hans Urs von Balthasar and Hans Küng.

A Book Finds A Publisher

Hardly arrived at home, I did what the Bonn theological faculty had feared twelve years before, and why it had tried to prevent my doctorate: I used the newly acquired platform to entirely revise my booklet of 1963 "On Celibacy of Priests of the Latin Rite", and to publish it now with more authority.

Within two weeks, I had collected and ingested all the newest literature on the topic – graciously tolerated by the members of the Albertus-Magnus-Institute –, and the draft of the book was finished within another fourteen days. Until the shell of the building had been replenished with notes and the text refined sufficiently, it still took, of course, some time, but the first fifty pages were really all as one piece.

Now, the lengthy process of examination through friends and experts began. Even more difficult was the business of finding a publisher for the manuscript.

The decisive public breakthrough for the small book was achieved by connections to the meanwhile deceased professor Richard Egenter in

Munich, an authority in Catholic moral theology of undisputed integrity, to whom I had listened in Munich as a student. Meanwhile, he had reached retirement age, yet often issued statements on topics of the day, for example in an article in the Jesuits' magazine "Stimmen der Zeit" (Voices of the Time) of September 1977 under the title "Considerations on Compulsory Celibacy," which was commented on in all church newspapers.

I sent him my manuscript and got the most comforting answer: "The study you sent was extremely appreciated," professor Egenter wrote, "because it offers the scientific substantiation of the arguments, which today are brought forward against compulsory celibacy, also by myself. I am therefore of the opinion that it must needs be printed." He had two doubts regarding some of my arguments that could be considered in the final draft of the manuscript.

At the end of his letter, Richard Egenter added: "A sincere, cordial God bless you, because you have undergone this great effort, in favour of our priesthood! I am confident that this labour of love will be rewarded, in any case by God himself." The certificate of Professor Egenter and the intercession of the church historian Professor Georg Denzler from Bamberg procured the acceptance of the book by the publisher Kösel-Verlag in Munich, on December 16, 1977.

Pastor Again

Although I had moderately calmed down in the Beuel apartment and had been capable to produce my celibacy-manuscript in continuous exchange with my wife, the legally ambiguous position, in which we were before the public – no longer priest and housekeeper, but also not husband and wife before civil law –, turned to be increasingly uncomfortable. On the other hand, I thought I would better live in an unassailable position, in the interest of the coming publication, so that the book would not be robbed of its effect because of foreseeable suspicions.

In autumn 1976, I sensed the desire to again participate in the cure of souls so strongly, that I asked the personnel manager of the diocese, prelate Schlafke, where there was a parish, in which I could help. In Villip, near Bad Godesberg, there was in fact a priest, who for years had asked for continuous help. So, at the end of October 1976, it was with great joy that I took on there a service which I continued to practice for two and a half years. The priest of nearly the same age as me wished that I should live in the parish, so in 1977 I had another change of residence, this time to Wachtberg-Villip.

That doesn't mean, however, that I had broken off with my wife. She had found an apartment with her daughter in the neighbourhood of Beuel. Our spiritual and mental connection had meanwhile become so strong through the common battle that I felt it to be a painful gap in the sincerity towards the parish in Villip, namely that I had to conceal my marriage before them. The good will to lay down this wall of concealing was there, I could however not wage the battle for a married priesthood before their eyes, I wanted to do it between the Curia and myself and neither involve the priest nor the communities.

An Attritional Feud Begins

The work on the book made good progress, and the near completion of the manuscript motivated me to make the Church have a look at my sacramental marriage. And so I engaged in a feud of attrition with the Cologne authorities, and even more so with the Vatican Curia. The validity of my sacramental emergency marriage was at stake, that is, a decision on the part of the church management, as to whether it was valid or not.

In January 1977, immediately after I had already sent a first version of my manuscript to Cardinal Höffner for examination, I applied for admission to a public blessing of our marriage on the basis of the submitted trains of thought, which proved the invalidity of the law of celibacy. After my letter dated January 27 had remained unanswered, I repeated my request on April 28, and received an answer on May 7, which did not address my real concern, however.

The letter signed by Cardinal Höffner reads as follows: "Dear Dr. Vogels! Thank you for your letters. Since the office of President of the German Bishops' Conference has brought me new tasks, it takes a while before I find the time to study longer manuscripts. Your explanations are untenable from the viewpoint of our Church. For, you presuppose that a Christian has a legal right to be ordained as a priest. There is no such a legal right. The Church has in fact laid down selection principles for the admission to priestly ordination. Such selection principles are, for example, the study of theology and the passing of the stipulated examinations, and furthermore the charisma of celibacy. The German Bishops' Conference has therefore issued the following statement: 'The fact that celibacy is a gift of grace from God for the sake of the kingdom of heaven does not forbid it from making it a selection principle for priestly service' (February 19, 1970). I sincerely ask you to abide by the order of the church, and remain with many greetings, Yours Josef Card. Höffner."

This was a fundamental comment by the Cardinal, which he strictly adhered to in the time to come. Yet, it suffers from at least two theological weaknesses: Firstly, I had not claimed a legal right for Christians to be ordained, but had spoken of the right of priests already ordained to the sacrament of marriage, according to 1 Cor 9:5. And secondly, the comment by the German Bishops' Conference is extremely problematic. Because if celibacy is a gift of grace from God for the sake of the kingdom of heaven, which in itself is not interconnected with priesthood, then the question is justified as from where the Church takes the right to make it a selection principle. If God even today calls priests in the Eastern Catholic Church not only from among celibate, but also among married men, must not the Western Church fear that it – to use a very strong picture – procures an abortion of priestly vocations in her womb, if it rejects candidates who are called to priesthood and marriage?

In this sense, I wrote to the Cardinal on May 13, and again on July 21. He answered on September 28, 1977: "It is prohibited for the bishop to ordain someone to priesthood, of whom the bishop does not have the moral certainty that God has given him the charisma of celibacy. The church is authorised to require this precondition."

Divine Right Versus Church Right

To demand that each candidate for ordination possesses the charisma of celibacy, ultimately means that the Western Church demands that *God* gives all priests the charisma. But can the Church dare to believe that God is at its disposal like this?

After the Cardinal had unequivocally established his position, it was plain that I could make no more progress here. I therefore tried to negotiate with the acting General Vicar, Hans Daniels (died 1992 at the age of 86). I sent him several letters and received an opportunity on December 10, 1977 to engage in a two-hour conversation with him alone.

The prelate had meanwhile read my manuscript. "The core of your book" – he said - "is probably the third chapter about the right to take along a woman. This may perhaps mean the wife, but you have completely exaggerated this right. Of course, there is the *human right to marriage*, but I can renounce that right, and the Church can establish such a renunciation as a condition."

"Therefore, the first chapter is also important," I answered, "one cannot abstain without having the *charisma* needed for this."

On this point, namely that one could only renounce the right to marry if one has the charisma of celibacy, we could agree. The prelate, however, continued immediately, that the church could select for the priesthood those, who have the charisma.

"You just said that the church establishes abdication of the right as a condition, now you say, it accepts only those who have the charisma" – I countered - "there you see the different reasons."

"They abstain, because they have the charisma."

"But the law never originated as a condition for admission, celibacy was simply *imposed* by law – '*lege impositus est*', as the Second Vatican Council still says in 1965 (Presbyterorum Ordinis N° 16). Nowhere are charisma and free will spoken of. Only since 1931 has an oath of free will been required. In the Middle Ages, the Church asserted celibacy with draconian measures, through enslavement of priest-wives, and in the year 1139 through the annulment of the priests' right to marriage, without asking for voluntary abdication on their side, and now releases priests from their service, because they cannot cope with abdication, for a lack of charisma. You see, it is nothing special with the free will, and not everyone is able to abdicate."

"I don't approve of the church's behaviour as you have just portrayed, either. I am also very much in favour of releasing priests from their duties, who have been ordained in ignorance of their abilities – similar to those ordained under fear and force, *vi et metu*."

"Why should they give up their vocation only because they cannot cope with celibacy?"

"This is something that not even the Eastern Church permits, namely that priests can marry after ordination," he replied. "Then you would have to say that the Eastern Church is also inconsistent."

"In the manuscript, I brought the late Patriarch Athenagoras of Constantinople to mind, who actually thought priests must be permitted to marry after ordination."

Daniels replied: "Anyway, you will find no official voice to acknowledge your position and to say: he is right."

I then asked what had been the result of the examination of my manuscript in the General Vicariate.

"It has not been finished yet," he answered. I replied: "It seems to me that you have not rejected the arguments of the manuscript by what you have said."

"That is simply impossible for me," he said. "I should have nothing to do the whole day but study the matter... It would perhaps be a good idea to ask retired professors to deal with it," he proposed.

"Then you would deem it best to publish the manuscript?"

"No, I wouldn't," he replied. "I must speak with the Cardinal once more, perhaps we can submit the manuscript, as it is, to the Congregation for the Doctrine of Faith."

From The Papal Court To The Congregation For The Doctrine Of Faith

Some days later, I sent the prelate a Latin abridgment to be presented in Rome, as he had suggested, in addition with my plea for being officially allowed to marry. The prelate told me on the phone that adding this plea was inopportune. The Cardinal himself, however, even refused to pass on the abridgment. He told me through the prelate that I should finally give up and keep quiet.

However, I neither gave in nor did I remain silent. On January 3, 1978, I addressed a petition directly to the highest papal court, the Rota Romana. My bishop, I wrote, had refused my request for official admission to a church wedding, without pondering my reasons from divine right. I called for help that I might get my right. If I spoke of my right, of course I always had the ulterior motive: my right, that I would like to push through on behalf of *all* priests called to marriage.

The Rota Romana had forwarded the complaint to the Congregation for the Doctrine of Faith, because it was responsible. So, I set out in order to see this Congregation. There, I had a conversation on March 21, 1978, with Monsignor Szertö, a Hungarian, who spoke German well and had processed my petition. I can reproduce this colloquy in full length, as I wrote minutes from memory the following day.

"The answer to the petition you sent to the Sacra Rota has already been sent to your archbishop. From there you will receive further information. We checked your premises and your conclusions. They were presented to a session of the Congregation. All were unanimously of the opinion that there was *plena evidentia* (it was absolutely clear) that your archbishop Cardinal Höffner was completely right when he declined your plea for permission to wed as a priest."

"And my appeal to 1 Cor 9:5, the divine right, did you read that?"

"Yes, I did. But it would be necessary to first check the context more exactly, which is the meaning of the term 'apostles' and of the other concepts. Maybe 'apostle' is used in another sense."

"But the apostles, who were meant, were mentioned by name!, Peter, the brethren of the Lord and the other apostles. Apostles are therefore thought of in the strictest sense."

"Anyway, your argument did not convince me. Don't be ungrateful to your Cardinal, as well. He fought for you in person for you to be admitted to celebrate Mass again. Thank God on your knees that you can celebrate again."

"That's what I do. Do you think I want to lose that again? But I don't think I must stop thinking because of this."

"What you think is utopia, a dream. Maybe, one day married men will be admitted to the priesthood. We are people who live today and will die tomorrow; we don't know how the Holy Ghost will lead the Church. But that priests can marry, never, I would walk through fire for that."

"Where should I turn then, in order to have the theoretical question examined, whether *ius divinum,* divine right, is at stake here? You are responsible in this Congregation for questions of faith."

"We have so much to examine here, why should we examine this question specifically? You can also turn to the Commission for the Revision of the Codex, to Cardinal Felici."

"Seriously, do you think that would be of any use?"

"No. If you had turned to theology, you would perhaps have got a different answer." So, as a theologian he indirectly said I was right. "Since you turned to the authority, the answer had to abide by the existing law."

Finally, Monsignor Szertö added: "It seems you are not content with my answer." – "I am content that you expect the Holy Spirit to lead the Church," I replied.

Deliberate Ignorance

So far the conversation which I first reported without comment. The contradictions are noteworthy. Monsignor Szertö first claimed that the Congregation had checked my premises, then however admitted that it must first check the context of the verse in order to be able to assess my appeal to the *ius divinum*. He was not even aware of the obvious contents of the passage.

It was obviously a case of thoughtlessness when the Monsignor refused to examine my findings on the part of the Congregation, which was responsible according to the opinion of the Rota. "Why should we?," he said, although the question had been officially submitted by the Rota! Moral theology calls such a stand an "*ignorantia crassa et affectata*" – deliberate and intentional ignorance.

Besides you cannot overlook the contradiction, namely that the Congregation responsible and competent for questions of principle, ranking above the current church law, apparently adjudicates only according to the current law. It had not been taken into account at all whether a higher ranking divine right, which is always in force, could possibly be at stake.

All in all one feels reminded of Jesus' word: "How clever you are, setting aside the commandment of God, in order to maintain your tradition" (Mk 7:9). The tactic was exactly the same here in Rome as that of the prelate in Cologne: When he couldn't reply with anything of further substance to my arguments, he referred to my duty of gratitude towards the authority. It was indeed exactly as the Cologne prelate had said: "You will find no voice in the hierarchy who will say you are right." Of course, if they were not even ready to examine the question!

Not much later, I received the Congregation's answer, sent via Cologne. It dated from February 9 and was addressed to Cardinal Höffner. Cardinal Franjo Seper, the prefect of the Congregation, reported to him that I had submitted an extensive composition on priesthood and the law of celibacy, and had remonstrated with the Holy See against his, Cardinal Höffner's, refusal of my request for admission to marriage. "As to the matter, I ask your Eminence, after we have properly pondered all the circumstances of the case, to make aware to the aforementioned priest in a friendly manner that the 'grievance' (*recursus*) we are dealing with, obviously cannot be stated, because it contravenes the current law of sacred celibacy."

Now I had it in black and white, namely that church law is the highest norm for the Congregation for the Doctrine of Faith and that the *ius divinum*, the higher ranking divine right of the Bible, is not even worth mentioning. In other words, that my appeal to it did not need to be refuted, but could simply remain ignored. This is all the more incomprehensible, since according to the standard commentary to the Codex Iuris Canonici by Adrian van Hove, Mechelen 1945, highly valued in Rome as well, the divine right is always in force and overrides church law, also without having been published by the church through ecclesiastical laws. That goes after all without saying, given the teaching of the Catholic Church on natural right sanctioned by the Creator and on divine right of the Sacred Scripture. It cannot be abrogated and is unsurpassable, because God in any case is above the Church.

I had been in an extensive correspondence with Hans Urs Wili, a Swiss lawyer on exactly this question, namely of whether divine right is actually in force in the church or only theoretically. We sometimes fought hard on whether the "legal rules" to be found in the Scripture and mentioned in canon 6 N° 6 of the code CIC of 1918 as "*ius divinum positivum*", positive divine right sanctioned by God, are truly enforceable or are just lip service of the present Code. Unfortunately, Herr Wili had first been proven right with his opinion of the just theoretical validity of *ius divinum* in the Western Church.

On April 29, 1978, in a Latin letter to the Congregation, I presented my view of the problem extensively and informed them that there was nothing left for me than to publish my manuscript and have the examination, done by the People of God as well as by theological science.

Therefore, it cannot be said that I had not tried everything to avoid a dispute in public and to deliver the litigation with the superiors behind closed doors. When perusing the files, one simply must conclude that the argument of the church authorities was not only weak, but evasive and incapable of shaking my conviction of the biblical right of priests to marriage anyway.

No Imprimatur for "Compulsory Celibacy"

I now pursued the publication of the manuscript with greater intensity, which had already been secured since December 16, 1977, however simultaneously undertook another attempt to make it appear in agreement with church authority.

On the occasion of a study week held in the old Bensberg seminary, where the Cardinal also showed up towards the end, I asked him for the Imprimatur for the book. The Cardinal did not want to decide it without the responsible adviser on questions of faith, auxiliary bishop Dr. Hubert Luthe. Fortunately, he lived in the same old seminar in Bensberg at that time, so I could submit the just printed proofs to him. He, in turn, saw himself unable to give the print his permission. He thought the book would "contravene the teaching of the church," he wrote in a note to me. I asked him by letter with which teaching it contrasted. His answer more or less said, it was in contrast to the discipline of the Church, which as everyone knows is not infallible. He later personally confirmed that not one of my sentences would contravene matters of belief, yet he regarded the publication as inopportune, because it would be exploited by the largely unbelieving public, and because it doesn't encourage wavering priests to remain celibate. I could only object that this was tragic in the view of those who want to keep up the law, it is a sign for me however, that the discipline must be changed.

In any case the auxiliary bishop offered to talk with the theological expert responsible for the Imprimatur for my book, Dr. Wilfried Paschen, about the first manuscript of 50 pages, which had been presented to him long ago. Meanwhile, Dr. Paschen (died 2004) had produced a five-page certificate, which had served as the basis for his own very fast judgment. I accepted the offer of a conversation gratefully.

The conversation on July 7 and 21, 1978, went quite favourably; minutes were drawn up and signed by both involved. Two sentences are crucial. At the end of the first date, Dr. Paschen said: "What seriously can be said and discussed should not be withheld either." That was practically equal to an expert certificate *for* the publication and revoked his prior No. At the end of the second conversation Dr. Paschen admitted: "The question of whether compulsory celibacy has a foundation in the essentials of Catholic faith can be posed." Thereby, the *content* of the question was also acknowledged as legitimate. Bishop Luthe later called it an intellectual pleasure to read the minutes; however it did not alter his decision to refuse the Imprimatur.

Refusal Of A Nullity Process

Irresistibly, I now felt driven to step out from the inner conflict of a priestly "double life". On one hand, my inner conviction that a divinely guaranteed right of priests to marriage does exist, was so established, that I saw no reason to wait any longer with the personal consequences to be drawn from this conviction, that is, with civil marriage. On the other hand, the church authority still made a stand against this conviction, *without* valid arguments, and forced me to hide my calling to marriage from the people for whom I was a priest.

Wasn't it an acceptable way to ask a church court to take a decision on my sacramental emergency marriage of 1974 through a nullity process? The then General Vicar Nettekoven had called this marriage null and void. But by church law it is he, who must prove the nullity, because in accordance with current church right, can. 1014 of the Codex Iuris Canonici of 1918, that is can 1060 CIC/1983, *marriage enjoys the protection of the right and is to be regarded as valid, until the opposite is proven by a process.* Until now, no such process had been made. If my appeal on the divine right was correct, not the invalidity but the validity of my marriage had to turn out in a process. And that without causing a sensation, in a quiet discussion of all arguments, before an official committee of the church.

For half a year, from June to December 1978, I repeatedly submitted this request, first to auxiliary bishop Luthe, then to the acting General Vicar Daniels. It always remained without answer, although such a request must, by right (Codex Iuris Canonici, can. 1709 f) be answered within a month.

Only on February 20, 1979, when the milk had long been spilt, did I get an answer from the acting General Vicar, who refused a nullity process with the remarkable reason, that there was no public interest in such a process. In person, he further told me that it was virtually "perverse", if I wanted an invalidity process not to lead to the proof of invalidity but the validity of a marriage! – Why should something positive be perverse, I wondered.

The Scandal Stays Away

At the end of August 1978, the book "*Pflichtzölibat*" ("Compulsory Celibacy") eventually appeared in the Munich based publishing house Kösel-Verlag, and surprisingly produced no scandal at all. On one hand, this was due to the fact that the promotional activities had not run full steam ahead, because of the gentlemen's agreement, which the publishing house and the Cologne General Vicariate had agreed to, after my request for the Imprimatur had failed. On the other hand the name of the author told the readers nothing.

So, only three major book reviews appeared. Professor Peter Hünermann, a theologian of the University of Münster, Westphalia, discussed my book in the magazine "Publik-Forum", after the "Theologische Revue" in Münster had refused to publish his review. A theological magazine also based in Brussels devoted considerable space to my theses, and my spiritual mentor Heinrich Spaemann wrote a review for the weekly "Christ in der Gegenwart" edited by the Herder-Verlag. Spaemann's review was offered in the publisher's article-service as an offprint, from which altogether 40,000 copies were ordered. However, that had no effect on the sale of the book.

In February 1979, another longer review finally appeared in the "Theologische Revue", where Professor Erwin Iserloh tried to disarm the argument of the small book. Now it was clear why the positive review by Hünermann had been refused. The review by Professor Iserloh obviously went back to the encouragement by bishop Luthe, who had told me candidly: "The feet of those who will carry you away are already at the door" (see Acts 5:9). After all, they considered it necessary to dedicate a four page editorial of the "Revue" on the refutation of my 127 pages! I cannot say Iserloh was successful in refuting me, especially since he frequently shortened my conclusions in his quotes, and above all had nothing to reply to 1 Cor 9:5, the right of the apostles to take along wives, the second mainstay of the thesis, the first being Matt 19:11 about the charisma necessary for celibacy.

Besides, through Hans Küng's intercession I was asked, by the magazine "Concilium", published in eight languages, to write an article on the basis of my book on "The Community's Right to a Priest in Collision with Compulsory Celibacy" (which appeared March 1980 in 'Concilium'), and due to this article my theses became internationally known and welcomed by married priests worldwide.

The further course of public discussion on the book did not interest me very much. I had considered the publication as such only a stopgap, because my main interest had been to convince the church superiors directly. All the more, the continuing in-fighting with the Cologne Church authority kept me busy, by which I hoped to have the right prevail through my own case.

Chapter 7
After The Matrimonial Yes - Excommunication

To take the next crucial step, I had to overcome several objections I had made to myself. In my book "Compulsory Celibacy" I had written that priests suffering from celibacy should not exploit their freedom to marry, until the invalidity of the law has been recognised by all. If I now tried to obtain myself the right to marriage, this seemed to be in contrast with my own admonition. I felt however bound not only to wait for the official acknowledgment of this right, but to further function as a pioneer, in order to pull the chestnuts of the concerned out of the fire. On no account did I want to encourage public disobedience. Furthermore, I actually hoped in naïve optimism to come to terms with my bishop. This hope was motivated by my unshakable belief that the Catholic Church which we confess in the Credo as an object of belief, has something to do with God and is reigned by him in ultimate authority. Therefore, the divine right would finally make its way all on its own – thus I thought. So, the third phase of the battle in this unequally armed conflict began.

The Attempt To Pull The Chestnuts Out Of The Fire

In the week before Christmas, I sent Cardinal Höffner a wholeheartedly trusting and, as I thought, also affectionate hand-written letter for Christmas Eve, December 24, which was at the same time his birthday. I wrote for example: As he, the Cardinal, and I, too with all our soul and all good will wanted to serve the same Lord, Christ, it ought to be possible that we meet in him and that the insights gained, which, as I firmly believed, came from God, would be heeded by the church leadership.

I had tried everything to get out of the awful dilemma of the tension between priesthood and marriage to one or the other side, and had spared no pains in doing so. Because of my negative experiences, the depressions, and the positive ones, the healing through the love of a woman, I now know for certain that the solution for me and many others would lie in the connection between priesthood and marriage. I therefore asked him, on the basis of my theoretical works on the apostles' right to take along wives, to advocate a general solution in this sense.

After Christmas, I attended a meeting of the sacerdotal fraternity Jesus Caritas, a member of the spiritual family of Charles de Foucauld, held every year at about this time in Leutesdorf on the Rhine. At this meeting, I took an important decision for my further action. What I had been commissioned with, since 1960, was to fight for the marriage of priests; and apparently civil marriage was also a part of performing this task. Only through the act of marriage at the registry office would I be in the situation "to be on my guard against the leaven of the Pharisees, I mean their hypocrisy," as the Lord says (Lk 12:1). Only by avowing myself to my marriage in public would I step out of the unintentional secrecy in which my emergency marriage had been lived until now, and would stop with all forms of hypocrisy. For this important step, February 2, 1979, seemed a suitable date, a feast of the Lord and of Mary, and at the same time the twentieth anniversary of my ordination.

Back home, I found the reply from the Cardinal, in which he wrote: "Dear brother! For your Christmas letter, which I read with emotion, I thank you very much. I am sorry that you are not able to abandon your topic." Then he repeated the comment by the hierarchy already known to me, namely that nobody has a right to ordination, and again added the sentence of the German Bishops' Conference of 1970: "The fact that celibacy is a gift of grace from God for the sake of the kingdom of heaven does not forbid it being made a selection-principle for priestly service."

The Cardinal had already quoted this sentence in May 1977 and I had already refuted it in my book 'Compulsory Celibacy' with biblical arguments. It was like a speech from a record, although it should be an answer from emotion to my cry for help he had obviously heard. As my confidence in him was disappointed, I responded in a manner that he could see, I was hurt.

I sat down and wrote this letter to the Cardinal. I alerted him to the fact that again he had not entered into the question as such, namely that priests already admitted and ordained, as successors to the apostles, even after ordination have the "right to take along wives," as attested by Paul. "The General Vicariate, I said, "has responded with silence to my repeated requests over many times, it might test the 1974 emergency church wedding for its validity." From this silence, I would conclude its consent, in accordance with the old principle: "*Qui tacet, consentire videtur*" – Silence gives consent.

I announced that I would finally make the civil wedding follow the church marriage, and added: "If the General Vicariate doesn't adopt an attitude with regard to it *before*, but answers with sanctions only *afterwards*, I will sue it before God and man because of insidiousness." That was sharp. I meant: if I am so fair as to announce my actions in advance, I could probably reckon with just as much fairness from their side.

Preparation For The Civil Wedding

I waited in vain for an answer over a whole month. In the meantime, I went to the registry office to fix the date for the wedding: February 2.

In the Benedictine Scheyern Abbey, the old-abbot Johannes Maria Hoeck had for years maintained his benevolence for me. The new abbot had invited me for a vacation in January, so that I could think quietly about everything. It was like a release from the tension, when for two weeks, from January 14 to 28, I was able to be a guest in Scheyern. There, all prayers and meditations of the first week in a "review of life" – the "révision de vie" practised by Charles de Foucauld and his spiritual family – induced me to understand that I should consistently finish the line which pointed from my depression in the Easter-Vigil 1952 and the heavier one in the year 1959 to the realisation that an imposed celibacy was unbearable for me, and finally from my gradual healing through marriage now to civil wedding.

No sooner had I decided with utmost inner certainty to proceed that way, I made several big mistakes. I would have had to speak with the confessor and submit my plan to his opinion. Then my wife, the abbot, finally the Cardinal should have been informed. Instead, I began by asking the marriage witnesses to take part in the wedding. After I had sent off the letters to these witnesses, at night the well-known cramp in the heart frightened me again, and I felt I had done wrong. During the day I again became bewildered, so that even prayer could no longer help. I finally escaped into the sentence, which I pronounced loudly to myself: "The decision has been taken, and that settles the matter!" Immediately, the bewilderment vanished.

Because a common home is a constituent part of marriage, I drove home for two days, in order to discuss everything with my wife and to rent an apartment, where we could move in after February 2.

Consent At The Registry Office

On the morning of February 2 at 6 o'clock, I celebrated Mass as usual with the sisters in Wahn, this time in the presence of my wife and my mother-in-law. It was the feast of Candlemas, at the same time the anniversary of my ordination twenty years ago. After breakfast, which the sisters had lovingly prepared for us, I drove with the two ladies in my car to the Cardinal's house in the Eintrachtstraße in Cologne. Although Renate and I had first thought it superfluous to inform the Cardinal once again, since the letter dated January 2 amply sufficed, I now handed over a letter to the secretary of the Cardinal as my superior. The letter had approximately the following content: For half a year, I had asked the General Vicariate and the Cardinal whether it is allowed or not for a priest to take along a wife, in accordance with 1 Cor 9:5, they however had kept silent; and just like Jesus at that time had not been kept off through the silence of the Pharisees from healing someone (see Mk 3:4), I now did not want to have myself kept off from being healed by Jesus, by exchanging our matrimonial Yes on February 2 at 11 o'clock before the registry office in Bonn-Beuel.

"I have an appointment at 11 o'clock," I said to the secretary, "I would like to let the Cardinal know in advance."

"But you know he is going to ordain priests in the Cathedral at 8 o'clock," he replied.

"Yes, I know. Then please give him the letter immediately afterwards."

Admittedly, even that was late for the Cardinal to react, if he had wanted to. Maybe, however there was something good in it, anyway. Certainly he would have tried to discourage me from the civil marriage, further years would have passed, which would have delayed my personal maturation, the tension would have become unbearable and the burden above all untenable for my wife. Enough: we *got* married on February 2, 1979, at 11 o'clock at the registry office in Bonn-Beuel. The witnesses were my brother and the sister of my wife.

In so doing, I now publicly professed my faith in the existence of the apostolic right of priests to be accompanied by a wife, guaranteed by the Lord and in force in the entire Church until 1054, the Great Schism, and until 1139, the Second Lateran Council, where compulsory celibacy was imposed from then on in the Western Churches only. At the same time, I avowed myself to my wife, who had accompanied me in all these difficult years, had made me emotionally capable to write the doctoral thesis, had pursued and corrected the celibacy book in all its stages and had "by the way" educated her daughter and managed the very responsible profession of an old people's nurse. That required a degree of mental strength and love which God had apparently given her, and which probably was the reason why he had brought us together. No human being can conceive what this woman went through and achieved regarding marriage for priests in the Catholic Church. For sure, this can be said of many other women, too, who helped a priest grow ripe and become healthy. In any case, I can say it of her, whom God has led to me.

Excommunicated And Dismissed Without Notice

In my good faith, I had believed, that if we refer to the divine right, nothing could happen to us. This right, I thought, must be a plank on which we could walk on the water. Yet, I already sensed the lurking depth on the wedding day, when suddenly in the middle of the family celebration, I had to think of "Cologne". Fear laced up my heart, but now there was no way back. In the morning, I had blessed the beautiful terraced house at the edge of a small forest in Bonn East, to which we wanted to move, and had been quite quiet since then. What had been prepared for so long and was supported by prayer, could not be wrong.

On February 13, the current General Vicar, to whom my letter to the Cardinal had been forwarded, already wrote that with immediate effect I could not say Mass any longer, we were both excommunicated.

"To avoid further measures, I ask you to come back from your erroneous path without delay," the General Vicar wrote. "No remark by our Cardinal can be reason for you to assume that he would agree with your actions." Admittedly not a remark, but his silence and that of the General Vicariate, had indeed given me this conviction. Silence also means consent under church law. Whether that was naïve on my side or not, it would have been the duty of the authority to warn me anyway, especially since I had announced my marriage and had asked what they, in turn, would do.

I agreed to a conversation with the General Vicar. It took place on February 16. The prelate revealed to me that the Cardinal had said: "I believe, we must make a cut."

I could make him understand that I had acted in subjective conviction of my right, therefore had not incurred the penalty due to a lack of evil intent and because I was not aware that my actions were wrong. As a result, he admitted that in the General Vicariate they had in fact for these reasons wondered, *whether they could punish me at all*; they had however then decided "for punishment of the *external act*," because marriage of a priest is after all something monstrous in itself.

I reminded the General Vicar that punishment of the exterior act without considering the *culpability* is something completely impossible according to civil and church law: "*Nulla poena sine culpa*" – "no penalty without guilt". Rather, it would have been the method of pure legal positivism, which in the totalitarian state of the "Third Reich" had led to such terrible consequences. After all, only a *guilty* person could be punished.

The General Vicar finally acknowledged my good intent in that I was striving for a reform of the law in the Western Church, appealing to the right of the Early Church and the Eastern Church, to the benefit of the Church and priests concerned, "under high personal commitment," as he literally said.

My previous letter to the Cardinal, dated January 2, in which I had definitely announced my step had not been forwarded to the General Vicar. As to why the Cardinal had kept silent to this letter, he knew only so much, namely that he had not taken my threat seriously, because I had previously made similar announcements, but had until now never acted accordingly. I, for my part, had assumed that he wanted to let me experiment and had therefore remained silent. So it turned out that both sides had fallen prey to a misunderstanding.

The General Vicar asked me to give him what I had said in writing and promised to talk to the Cardinal about the whole affair once more.

Yet as soon as he had my written report of our conversation in his hands, he answered that he could not go into the details of my explanation, since this would not contribute to clarifying my situation. Since I had not been ready to come back from my erroneous path instantaneously, that is to get divorced again, I was excommunicated, *irregular*, and in addition dismissed without notice from the Albertus-Magnus-Institute. – If this is not monstrous, what is? The Church deliberately punished an innocent person!

As soon as this letter arrived at the new apartment, an icy breath already spread from its envelope; and as I got to read the words "excommunicated," "not allowed to," "dismissed without notice," black on white, the news passed like a sting through my heart.

Of course, I appealed in Rome against the notification by the General Vicar, who had not taken into account my justification from the divine right – it was of no use. The Papal Nuntius in Bonn somewhat later, on May 5, 1979, notified me that the Congregation for the Doctrine of Faith had "not accepted" my appeal. Reasons were not given. I wondered – and still ask myself today: Is the Church that once called itself a *societas perfecta*, a "perfect society", is the Vatican not even a government under law?

The Press Reports

The Archdiocesan General Vicariate sent the parish I served in the following communication, which was printed in the parish letter of the Catholic parish of St. Simon and Judas of Wachtberg-Villip:

"Dr. Heinz-Jürgen Vogels, who has until now cooperated in the parish Wachtberg-Villip, married at the registry office in Bonn-Beuel on February 2, 1979. He has thereby made it impossible for any further priestly activity. We regret this step by Dr. Vogels. Unfortunately, we failed to succeed in holding him back from this step."

This way of representing things hit me deeply. It didn't correspond to the facts. On my announcement of January 2, the General Vicariate had done nothing to discourage me from this step! After reading this letter with the parish priest, I asked him to accept a correction for the parish letter in writing or to read it out. Since he was not ready to do so, I quickly decided to go to the Bonn post office and use the public teleprinter to tell the General Vicar: "If you haven't corrected the objectively untrue assertion that you tried in vain to hold me back from civil marriage, I feel impelled to have it corrected through the newspapers. I urgently ask you to avert damage from the community of Villip and to inform it of the objective truth, including the motives for my action".

Friedrich Schiller rhymed in his drama 'The Piccolomini' (1800): "Das eben ist der Fluch der bösen Tat, dass sie fortzeugend Böses muss gebären" – that is the curse of evil deed: it must engender further deed. Lies were in fact added to condemning an innocent.

The required correction was not made. The Cologne authority later pleaded that it had already tried for years to discourage me from my thoughts. So, nothing was left for me than to hand over to Bonn's press corps a statement on the reasons for my marriage.

"General Vicariate forbids Dr. Vogels from exercising priestly office. Reason: marriage – not prepared to divorce." Under this heading, the Bonn-based General-Anzeiger of March 12, 1979, reported my case in a two column article.

Besides the comment by the Archdiocesan General Vicariate, the newspaper also informed its readers about how Villip's parish priest, Werner Sulk, responded and wrote in the parish letter: "Not a few of our community have come to appreciate Dr. Vogels during his service in our parish for more than two years as a devout and eager priest. We all, particularly those who have known him more closely, are deeply affected by this development. The Archdiocesan General Vicariate could not respond and act otherwise, because the Church only knows laicisation, i.e. the reduction of a priest to the lay state, which makes marriage possible, not however the marriage of a priest in office. In his conscience, Dr. Vogels believes he acted correctly. We thank him for the good work he did here, hopefully it will not be undone by his present action. He has left the community, we don't release him from our prayers. We must learn anew, again and again to live in a church of one faith, in which different opinions, saints and sinners, healthy and sick persons were always there."

Finally, the General Anzeiger gave its readers notice of my view of the affair: "The General Anzeiger is in receipt of a comment in which Dr. Vogels makes known that his marriage is based on the word of the apostle Paul: 'Do we perhaps not have the right to take along a sister in faith as wife, as the other apostles, the brethren of the Lord and Kephas (Peter)?'

Peter was married like most of the apostles. Dr. Vogels has been fighting for the acknowledgment of this right in the Catholic Church of the West for 19 years now. On January 1, 1974, he married in a sacramental emergency marriage, which he has, however, not lived according to his own statement, in order to be able to remain in the priestly service.

"Since August, he has asked Cologne's church leadership to impeach the emergency marriage by means of a nullity-process. Yet, nothing happened. Even as he told the Cardinal, he regards this marriage as valid and would let the civil wedding follow, no objection has taken place. Cologne's General Vicariate only took the trouble to persuade him to divorce *after* the marriage. He has, however, not followed this advice, in order not to play with the sacrament of marriage. The consequence was that Dr. Heinz-Jürgen Vogels was prohibited from exercising priestly functions according to church law. He filed an appeal against it at the Holy See on March 6. He thereby draws on the right of the apostle Paul, quoted above."

A Walk Through The Desert

When I paid a visit to the parsonage of Villip during this time and did not find the priest, I had a conversation with his housekeeper. The benign old mistress told me something at this opportunity which deeply touched and pleased me at the same time. She had been asked by several parishioners how it could be explained that a man, who obviously prayed much, could take this step and thereby put his profession at stake. She said that as a result of reading the "Sieve of Satan" – my first autobiographic records, which she had received from someone – she had replied: "I believe that with his battle he wants to clear a way for others, which does not yet exist." Without knowing further parts of this report, she had intuitively grasped the essential content of what I had regarded as my mission, and still do. She had always sensed that I was "different from the others" with whom she had to deal in the parsonage. Now, it had found its explanation of how and why I was different.

She also predicted that I would lose the security I had during the time of my battle. And so it was. The year 1979 became a walk through the desert. Without any vocational activity, gnawed by permanent doubts as to whether I had acted correctly, excluded from receiving holy communion, from the brothers, from the communities, sometimes as if physically and emotionally paralysed, incapable even to provide essential help in the household, only by insistent prayer, daily meditation before the tabernacle, and later by taking holy communion in foreign parishes could I keep my head above water.

Twice I succeeded in forcing the General Vicariate to continue the alimony for another quarter. I made a pilgrimage to Kevelaer on foot with Bonn's Kevelaer fraternity, from where my mental battle had taken its beginning – and to my surprise met Cardinal Höffner there. I got an audience with him in Cologne, and even got his agreement to pass on a seven-page letter to Pope John Paul II. This letter contained the essential findings of my book. But all that could not improve my mental situation.

The Cardinal, too, obviously suffered under the current situation. Moving letters in this time had passed back and forth, but I could not accept the unreasonable demand, either to divorce immediately or to ask for dispensation, which earlier had already not given me any relief. Only two months after my marriage, on April 17, did the Cardinal express himself regarding my continuous appeal to 1 Cor 9:5. The interpretation "wife" was admittedly the "most obvious one", but one could not necessarily limit the expression "woman" to this meaning. In my answer of April 23, I pointed to the "cloud of witnesses" (Hebrews 12:1) among the Early Fathers, who all offer the interpretation wife: Tertullian, Clement of Alexandria, Hilary of Poitiers, Jerome. The Cardinal, in fact, forwarded this letter and my enclosed letter to the Pope with an approving accompanying letter to Rome. But neither the Cardinal himself nor I ever received an answer to this letter! One is tempted to think of the words of St Paul in Romans (1:8): "Divine wrath will be revealed from heaven on all the impiety and wickedness of humans who in their wickedness suppress the truth."

The oases in the desert were my experiences in prayer: the certain feeling that God through marriage would finally let me come to my true self. To describe this new condition of truthfulness before God, many words came to mind: complete – calm – frank – relaxed – uncramped – honest – realistic – integrated – redeemed – in peace - be the one I really am.

Nevertheless, the walk through the desert continued un-changed and consumed my forces and resources.

Chapter 8
Taking Another Direction

I sent all possible offers of compromise to Cologne. I offered a life lead like brother and sister, spatial separation, even a divorce of the civil marriage, of which the sacramental marriage would have remained untouched, until to a plea for clarification of the legal question in Rome. I could not and did not want to give up the priesthood.

A letter from the General Vicar, which made further negotiations impossible, caused a move into quite another direction.

"You May Bend Me, But Not Break Me!"

The letter from the General Vicar dated July 23, 1979, informed me that for a return into the ministry and annulment of my excommunication not only did I need a divorce, but also a declaration of repentance, stating that I had contravened "the prohibition enacted by the church" in can. 2388, § 1 of the old CIC. The superiors required from me the remorse without previously having executed or ordered any serious examination of whether I was right in dwelling on the divine right, in other words whether actually divine, paramount right is given in 1 Cor 9:5, which takes the legal basis away from the church's prohibition and justifies my action.

The Cologne authority's way of proceeding was legally untenable. Also, a superior cannot require that his subordinate disavows his conviction. Even the II. Vatican Council says that (*Dignitatis humanae, N° 2*): "In religious matters nobody must be forced to act against their conscience nor be hindered in doing so." Here, the limit had been reached, up to where I was allowed to be loyal. Everything for which I had fought in the name of all priests called to marriage, and my belief in the divine right of 1 Cor 9:5, would I have to abandon for the sake of a human prohibition, which too clearly carried at its front the mark of the prophesy by the apostle Paul in 1 Tim 4:1-3, to be an erroneous "prohibition of marriage" from somatophobic, demonic teaching. The request to pretend remorse, where I could have none and was not allowed to have, repelled me.

From this day on, I was interested in the Old-Catholic Church, founded in 1870 after the first Vatican Council and represented above all in Germany, Switzerland and the Netherlands. In this church I could remain a priest and connect priesthood and marriage. So far, I had always refused to take such a step, because I did not only want to relieve my personal fate, but wanted to help prepare a *general* solution in the Western Catholic Church. Yet, as they wanted to break my moral backbone, I saw no possibility of remaining in community with the Roman Church. Pope John XXIII. had also said: "*You may bend me, not break me!*"

At the beginning of October 1979, as I returned from another unsuccessful visit to Rome via Assisi, I paid a visit to Spello near Assisi, where Carlo Carretto, one of the "Little Brothers of Jesus," kept his fraternity open for all, as a place of meeting in work and prayer. Carlo on exactly the day before I arrived had finished an article "Priest-shortage, a wrong problem." He pointed to the multiplicity of vocations among family-fathers which he found at his lectures and prayer vigils in Italian parishes. We both regarded it as a sign of the divine providence of the Lord that he had brought us together at exactly this moment, so that we could fortify and confirm each other.

Finally, even the last hope shattered, which had kept me back from taking the planned step: Cardinal Höffner had earlier told me, in May 1979, that he wanted to obtain an audience for me with Pope John Paul II; on November 14, 1979 he told me, however, that "an audience with the Holy Father is unfortunately not possible".

Moving Over To The Old-Catholic Church

Afterwards, I regarded it a great mistake to have left the community of the Roman Catholic Church on my own initiative, because *here* is the battlefield that had been assigned to me, and I later remedied this mistake.

At that time, however, the decision to go over to the Old-Catholic Church, apart from being repelled, originated from my burning wish to further participate in the proclamation of God's word.

In May 1980, an opportunity opened to become active full-time in the service of the Old-Catholic Church. At the beginning of the new year 1980, the Cologne Archdiocesan authority paid me only half my previous salary. So I had to look for another paid activity. Thanks to the kindness of bishop Brinkhues of the Old-Catholic Church (died 1995) and the relevant professor, I found a position as a part-time scientific assistant at the Old-Catholic Seminar of the University of Bonn, situated not three steps from the Albertus-Magnus–Institute, without needing to immediately give up my membership of the Roman Catholic Church. In April, things had developed so far that I believed I could not remain in the community of the Roman Catholic Church, which seemingly did not want to accord me, as almost all priests called to marriage, the right to live according to our conscience. Because, I now kept calm with this thought, the next day I went to the district court and declared that I seceded from the Roman Catholic Church, and then immediately entered the Old-Catholic Church. This step had only fiscal meaning for me, since my conscience seemed to approve it now. As regards the Church, it was actually only a change into another parish, as the Old-Catholic founders understood it, and a new incorporation into the personnel diocese (in contrast to a territorial diocese) of those who in 1870 had been excommunicated for the sake of their conscience. They could not agree to papal infallibility. They saw and see themselves as an emergency church. In accordance with the doctrine of the second Vatican Council on the church in Lumen gentium N° 14-16, also the non-Roman Churches belong to the Church of Christ.

For my psyche, and despite all the remaining mourning over the loss of community with the previous brothers, it was a gradual liberation finally to be cherished as a priest *and* husband. For my mind, it was a refreshment, finally to have to study another problem than that of celibacy, namely papal infallibility. Here, I believed to be able to serve the Church again in a different way. My application of December 18, 1979, to turn Old-Catholic contained the express intent "to work for the unity of the Church." That's what I did: I had continuous correspondence with Roman authorities.

In the course of studying the infallibility question, I discovered that the "Old-Catholic" interpretation, which the bishops of the minority at the first

Vaticanum had given to the decrees of July 18, 1870, has been generally accepted today by Catholic theology: The Pope must consult the Church *before* a definition, even if not *afterwards*.

Excommunicated For A Second Time

Of course, Cologne's General Vicariate, following the communication of my secession in April, stopped paying my alimony in May 1980, and I, moreover, incurred a second excommunication – because of my "secession from the faith." This pained me anew and persuaded me to pay a visit to the General Vicar.

Friendly as always, he could however show me no way of how I could remain in the Roman Catholic Church without denying my conviction.

As a second activity, beside the part-time work in the seminar, I was assigned in May 1980 to the task of arranging the episcopal archive in Bonn. By December, I had arranged the files of the diocese and the literary legacy of the first bishop Josef Hubert Reinkens and of Ignaz von Döllinger. In 1981, the German Research Foundation DFG awarded a stipend for the publication of the letters exchanged between Döllinger and Franz Heinrich Reusch, who in 1885 had published two important volumes on the Roman "*Index of prohibited books*", which indeed prepared its eventual abolition in 1967. The edition of the letters was confided to me under supervision of the Old-Catholic professor and in cooperation with the main editor of Döllinger's letters, professor Victor Conzemius in Lucerne.

"God's Honour Through The Healed Man..."

One of the most moving experiences I was granted in the marriage, now publicly known, was the solution of the tongue in prayer. During the spiritual exercises of 1959 before the ordination, my voice in private prayer of the breviary had suddenly fallen silent. Until then, I had always prayed with a low voice. From then on, I could only "read" the breviary. The jubilation had grown mute. This was a sign of extraordinary psychological significance, as I recognise today. No longer could I thank God, because something in me that wanted to live, had been sentenced to death by the final obligation to celibacy. A central psychic function was touched, the permission to engage in human love. I then suspected nothing of these aspects. But isn't it an unusually significant confirmation of my diagnosis that I, like so many other priests, cannot support celibacy, if I could again pray loudly in the very moment I was allowed to live completely again?

"God's honour through the healed human is the goal of creation," Ireneus of Lyon said. Should it not open the eyes of all those responsible in the church, if I, like so many others, have reached this goal as a married priest? Are they truly right, if they defame marriage, a sacrament instituted by Christ, by calling a priest who makes use of this sacrament, a criminal and excluding him from the community of believers? In condemning priests who marry, the church-leadership cannot refer to 1 Tim 5:11: "Do not admit younger widows to the roll, for *if* they are distracted from Christ, they want to marry again, and so are guilty of breaking their earlier vow to him," because the reason why younger widows should not be admitted to the roll of widows was that it is just normal for younger widows to want to marry again. Rather, the disciple of Paul writing here with the authority of the apostle "wishes that young widows should marry again, have children, and manage a household, so that they can give the enemy no occasion for invectives" (1 Tim 5:14).

In the same way, the church leadership should not want to impose celibacy on young men, because it is just normal for young men wanting to marry, and because their secession from the obligation gives occasion for blasphemy. Reason for the "guilt" which young people then incur is – again according to the witness of the first Letter to Timothy – not the individual Christian, but the church leadership, who expect too much of such young people. "Do not admit younger widows," it said at that time; "do not commit younger men to celibacy," would be the corresponding demand for the representatives of the Church today. One cannot repeat often enough: The ability to live in celibacy for the sake of heaven is based on a *charisma*, a particular gift of grace (Matt 19:11; 1 Cor 7:7). Those who have this gift will live in celibacy, even without a law. Those who do not have it are expected to do too much.

What Is Really Missing

In an endeavour to not only accuse the church leadership but to look also for my share in the events, I wrote several letters to Cologne and Rome, aimed at inner reconciliation at least.

After a long wait, I had the joy that Cardinal Höffner re-sponded to my letter on December 29, 1980, with these words.

"Honourable Dr. Vogels! For your Christmas and Birthday wishes I thank you very much. I see therein a sign that you don't want to tear off the ties, even though you left our Church. As I wrote, I have no longer understood your behaviour for approximately two years. I fought personally for you, namely that the celebration of the holy Mass was again made possible for you. Your thoughts and actions in the recent years have disappointed me. As far as priestly celibacy is concerned, there seem to be almost insurmountable language difficulties between us. You don't understand the Pope, who in the Cathedral of Fulda on November 17, 1980 said: 'Have heart and hands free for the friend Jesus Christ, be undivided there for him and bring his love to all: that is a witness, which in the first moment is not understood by all.' God may illuminate and lead you in 1981. That's what I wish for you from all my heart. Yours Joseph Cardinal Höffner."

These words were obviously lovingly chosen and seemed to seek inner reconciliation. Three further letters to the Cardinal followed, which however altered nothing about the situation.

I told the Cardinal that I didn't lack an understanding of the words of the Pope, but the charisma of celibacy. Biblically speaking, it should be put better: "Have heart and hands free for the friend Jesus Christ is a witness that not all can give, because it is not given to all." Prayer, too, could not alter anything about it, I wrote. Through the will to keep celibacy I had suffered a huge cramp, reaching down into the body, and now quite gradually by marriage had I been conducted into a deep serenity and inner peace, for which I thanked God.

An Important Discovery

While working on an article, I made an important discovery: In a certain distinction of the old "Corpus Iuris Canonici", the Canon Law book of the Church in force from 1142 to 1918, I found a quotation from 1 Cor 9:5! The distinction interprets this verse as the right of the apostles "to take along their wives," *uxores circumducere*, just as I did. The weight of this interpretation both in the exegetical and in the legal tradition of the church could only be assessed now, after my sights for the church of the first millennium had been sharpened through the Old-Catholic Church. The distinction of the "Corpus" dealt with the marriage of priests in East and West.

In the controversies resulting in the tragic division of 1054 between East and West Church, indeed even married priests played a role. Remarkably, at that time they were acknowledged from both sides! Only the question was debated as to whether priests were allowed to continue their marriage after ordination, that is could have matrimonial intercourse. The East approved it, Cardinal Humbert of Silva Candida, the legate of Pope Leo IX, condemned it. The spokesperson of the East in the dispute was Niketas, abbot of Studiou monastery in Constantinople. Against the position of Cardinal Humbert, he cited the "*apostolic canon*" N° 5, which was probably only written down in the 4th century: "No bishop, priest, deacon may dismiss his wife from his care on the pretext of piety. If he dismisses her, he shall be deposed" (*Migne, Patrologia Latina* 143,981D).

The representative of the West Church, Humbert, answered, that he acknowledged this canon: "We absolutely confess that bishop, priest, deacon, or subdeacon are not allowed to dismiss their respective wife (*propriam uxorem*) from his care for reasons of piety, but he should pass food and clothing to her. He shall, however, not lie with her in carnal lust, as he earlier used to do (*non ut ex more cum illa carnaliter iaceat*). So, we read the holy apostles have done, as says the blessed Paul: Do we not have the right to take along with us a sister (in Christ) as a wife (*uxores circumducere*), as the other apostles and the brothers of the Lord and Cephas?" (1 Cor 9:5). See, you fool, that he has not said 'to embrace', but 'to take along,' namely that she, too, should receive her livelihood from the wage for the sermon, not however, that between them the carnal marriage continued" (*Migne, Patrologia Latina* 143,997D).

This passage in Humbert's letter with the two quotations was inserted by Gratian into his 'Decretum Gratiani'. Gratian was a monk, who in the first half of the 12th century lived in Bologna and with his compendium of laws created the basis for Canon law. His "Decretum" since then has been part of the "Corpus Iuris Canonici", the letter can be found there as Distictio 31 caput 11 (*edition by Friedberg* I,114). This means nothing less than that at least up to the year 1054, when the letter just mentioned was written, East and West agreed on the right of priests to be married, on the basis of the apostolic right 1 Cor 9:5, and that the "woman" in this verse means "wife", *uxor*; only the type of marriage was in dispute, carnal or more economic. The highest authority, that there is in the Church, the papal authority, whose legate Humbert was, thereby confirmed the interpretation "wife of the apostles" as the right one, and at the same time he showed the undeniable significance of the passage for later church law, as the model of a married priesthood. Teaching and practice of the whole first millennium of the undivided Church are thus documented as being unanimous about their legitimacy! Can anything be brought forward that challenges the validity of this acknowledgment of the apostolic right of priests, written in papal commission?

The conclusions Humbert draws from "to take along", namely that it is not to "embrace," is acknowledged as contemporaneous today. The practice of Eastern Rite priests continuing their marriage after ordination was acknowledged by the Vatican Council II in 1965 as legitimate: "In the Catholic Eastern Rite churches there are priests of great merit in the conjugal state" (*Presbyterorum Ordinis* N° 16). Thus, it is clear that a married priesthood was the general property of the Catholic (that is, universal) Church for a thousand years, the West Church, however, which had done away with it since 1139, reveals a deficit in being Catholic, all-embracing.

In Chevetogne and Cluny

In March 1981, when on a skiing vacation in Switzerland, I made the Monsignor, who had passed my seven-page letter of 1979 on to the Pope together with the recommendation by Cardinal Höffner, aware of this important discovery. I did it in a letter to the pope, and received confirmation that my letter "has reached its destination."

In the course of the year, I again felt increasing unrest to do something that the nightly palpitation wanted from me. Since I could not find out what it was, I planned, with the approval of my wife, to do spiritual exercises during my annual vacation, and that in the monastery of Chevetogne, where the monks celebrate liturgy in the Eastern as well as the Western rite. The year before, I had, in this monastery, given exercises for the Old-Catholic students of theology.

Here, it took a peculiar turn. I read Paul's letter to the Romans, meditated on it, prayed much. After two days, I was sure to have to travel to Rome, although I had wanted to spend fourteen days in Chevetogne.

Crucial to this decision was the news I had heard shortly before, the revision of the Code of canon law in force since 1918, the "*Codex* Iuris Canonici", was near to conclusion. I worried that they would take the old law of celibacy unchanged and put it in the new Code, and thus cement it for the next generation. So, I believed I should try the utmost with my weak resources to prevent it.

It was hard for me to get my "sudden" decision across to the friendly host father. Likewise I had difficulty leaving the spiritual atmosphere of praying and meditating so quickly. Anyway, I safeguarded myself in Bonn against a possible decision error by asking my Old-Catholic bishop Josef Brinkhues, whether he had anything against my plan to drive to Rome on behalf of the law of celibacy. No, he had full trust in me, he replied. I had worked scientifically on the issue, it was therefore my very own matter, and if I did achieve something – which he thought not to be very likely –, then I would also have achieved something in favour of the legitimacy of the Old-Catholic Church's reform. This Church introduced the marriage of priests long ago in 1878. Therefore, I departed with the blessing of the bishop.

In Chevetogne, I had discovered something else. As my wife and I, some years ago, had been in Taizé near Cluny, I had missed the opportunity to visit the remains of the most famous monastery of the early Middle Ages, Cluny, from which the Saint of my birthday, Gregory VII, had come forth. From Cluny he had conquered Rome for his reform ideas, including the rigorous enforcement of priestly celibacy, which he began in 1074. Now, I wanted to make up for the neglect and did a detour via Cluny.

The gigantic size of the convent church, which had been the biggest church of Christianity from the 11th up to the 16th century – before St Peter's Cathedral in Rome was built –, made some of the self-confidence of the monks, who lived here even geographically in the centre of the West, dawn on me. With the Cluniacensian reformers, monkhood had finally taken over the management of the church, and it seems they had wanted to organise the whole church on the basis of their own rare charisma, against the model of a gigantic cloister. Obedience, asceticism, celibacy were, for them, self-evident values, which could only turn into a danger for the balance of the church through the force, by which they were imposed on others. The fullness of Catholic truth, that there are other charismas as well, sacramental marriage, the family community, reverence for the creation, had to suffer from it.

Only somewhat later, at the second Lateran Council of 1139, was the sacramental character of marriage defined, even if not for priests; before, the Church had therefore not yet realised marriage as a Christian value. So, it is only the historical situation of the Middle Ages which can explain why God permitted the one-sidedness of the monastic reform: the medieval feudalism threatened to fetter the clergy with terrestrial shackles through its system of churches owned by the nobility. Priest fathers could pass on the beneficium of their parish as an inheritance. The monks wanted to free the priesthood from the hands of the big landowners and the political powers. Church-historian Professor Victor Conzemius, teaching in Lucerne, whom I visited on my way to Rome, pointed it out to me.

The Codex Is Being Revised

Upon my arrival in Rome, I was able to arrange a date for the following day, July 28, 1981, in the Commission for the Revision of the Codex. Meanwhile, I inquired in the Secretariat of State, what had happened to my letter to the pope of March 1981. Of course, the Monsignor did not want to give me any information on all the steps taken. He said, I must be content if my arguments "accumulate with others arriving from around the world and thus eventually contribute to a decision." After all, I learned that I had been understood: "Yet you present the matter in such a way that there is no leeway left for the Pope to decide," added the Monsignor. Right: if 1 Cor 9:5 is a matter of *ius divinum*, a right enacted and guaranteed by God, then the Pope cannot but accede to this right.

In the Commission for the Revision of the Codex Iuris Canonici, I had to do with the Spanish Monsignor Herranz on the next day, who later was nominated a bishop. Herranz devoted one hour to me and listened alertly. I asked him whether the Commission had considered the possibility that 1 Cor 9:5 is a matter of divine right, so that an opposing celibacy regulation contradicted the personal God-granted freedom of the individual priest to marriage. He answered the first question in the affirmative, and said to the second, one must assume that the Council has answered in the negative. Never before, he said, had celibacy been under debate in as much detail as during the Second Vatican Council, even if on demand of the Pope not in public.

He gave me, however, some information which was of crucial importance, namely that the Council had, under assistance of the Holy Spirit recognised "the non-identity of the two charisms of priesthood and celibacy" (*"la non-identità delle due carismi"*), and *that* was why the Council had formulated, in the Decree on Service and Life of Priests, that celibacy "is not required by the very nature of priesthood" (*non exigitur quidem a sacerdotio suapte natura*: *Presbyterorum Ordinis* N° 16), it does therefore not necessarily belong to the priesthood.

This insight had never before been conveyed to me: The Council's word, he said, were inspired by the Holy Spirit, who worked a cognition, which I had won under most difficult circumstances: "The calling to priesthood is not identical with the charism of celibacy." Thanks be to God that through my first manuscript of 1963 "On Celibacy of Priests of the Latin Rite", I had been of some help for this realisation of the Council! When the Council had started, I had sent it to all the German bishops. One of them, Cardinal Döpfner from Munich, on the basis of this manuscript, had pronounced the truth of the distinct charisms of priesthood and celibacy in the Council audience on October 1965. I can assume that, because I earlier told that after reading my booklet he wrote his priests a letter stating that he had "recently given much thought to celibacy." The fact of Döpfner's speech is mentioned in the supplement to the "Lexikon für Theologie und Kirche", covering the Council, volume III, page 220 note 21. But why had the Council not been consistent enough to draw the consequences from this insight? If the two charisms of priesthood and celibacy are not identical, it should have separated priesthood from celibacy legally as well.

The next day, I reminded Monsignor Herranz of this Council insight in a letter and told him that the Holy Spirit, speaking through the Council, had already procured a theoretical separation of priesthood and celibacy; if we followed him along this path, we would arrive at the practical separation of the two callings, that is, at the free choice of priests between marriage and celibacy, depending on the charisma they receive. At least my visit in Rome had made it clear: Everything has been prepared theoretically for this free choice. Enactment is wanted!

Return Into The Roman Church

I had only been in the Old-Catholic Church for two years. My request of May 1982 to be again accepted into the Roman mother-church had several reasons. On one hand, certain developments in the Old-Catholic Church induced me to do so, and on the other, also my longing for Catholic worship, the reading of Cardinal Newman, and, above all, the discovery that in the theological literature of these days my thesis published in "Pflichtzölibat" (Compulsory Celibacy, 1978), that one could not extort the charisma of celibacy from God, was simply brushed from the table – for instance by Gisbert Greshake in his book "Being a Priest". If I wanted to join in the inner-Catholic discussion, I told myself, I had to come back to the old battlefield.

The conditions for a return were extraordinarily tough. To be absolved from the double excommunication, I had of course to leave the Old-Catholic Church. I did that in June 1982. On the other hand, I should submit also a plea for dispensation of celibacy, so that my marriage could be "arranged in church order".

Admittedly I was aware that I must once more give up the exercise of my priesthood for a longer time. In spite of this willingness, I could not come to terms with renouncing my priestly vocation, which was demanded if I wanted dispensation. If I did not obtain certainty of whether the right of the apostles to take along wives was a divine right or not, I could not renounce, because a legal claim to marriage *as a priest* could always be derived from it, I wrote to Cologne's General Vicariate, on June 23, 1982. In the same letter I asked for a decision on this from Rome.

The General Vicar invited me to see him on August 11, and he revealed to me that neither for the Cardinal nor for him was it a question of whether or not *ius divinum* is contained in St Paul's statement. They would not ask the Vatican such a question. That might be different for me, but Rome would not answer private persons, that was simply not usual.

Again, one can ask: Why did the bishop not act on behalf of a priest of his diocese? This was a dispute in which the subordinate saw a God-given privilege speaking in his favour, the superior however not. If the subordinate for his part was not entitled to go to the responsible committee, it would have been the duty of the superior to bring the dispute before the higher authority.

The General Vicar admitted that my question had approximately the rank of an inquiry at the papal Bible Commission, as to whether the Pentateuch, the first five books of the Old Testament, originated from Moses or not. – But if he had recognised the significance of this question, why then did he not pass it on?

As a last resort, I was allowed – on my request – to once again have a conversation with the former expert on my book "Compulsory Celibacy," Dr. Wilfried Paschen. This discussion proceeded very well. We reached total agreement: "The habit, that the apostles went into the communities together with their wives, was covered by the authority of the Lord", say the minutes of this conversation of September 8, 1982. That is, the will of the Lord is behind the factual custom of the apostles to take their wives with them into the mission field. My inquiry was nevertheless not referred to Rome. May anyone take a positive judgment on this behaviour, I can't.

Civil Divorce

In November 1982, I finally sent a plea for dispensation to the Vatican, which contained my express wish "to further practice my priestly vocation; I believe I am entitled by divine right to do so". The protocol of the conversation of September 8, 1982, with Dr. Paschen was enclosed. In April 1983 I received an answer from Rome, via the Cologne Curia: once more it did *not address* the issue of the theoretical, biblical problem of divine right. Instead I was asked to "renounce my priestly rights or authorities unambiguously," or if this were too difficult for me, "to dissolve the matrimonial community" with my wife, as literally stated in the letter dated April 12, 1983. That is, the Church demanded us to divorce.

Since neither Cologne nor Rome had adjudicated, whether I have a *divine right* to remain in the priesthood as a married man, a request for *dispensation* would again have meant the disavowal of my conviction of being allowed to be a *priest and* a husband at the same time. So, in January 1984, I finally took the path of civil divorce, in order to be firstly absolved from the excommunication, and then hopefully to be readmitted to the priesthood. I was able, even though with great difficulty, to convince even my wife of taking this step: Our *sacramental* emergency marriage of 1974 should *not suffer from this tactical retreat*. Our church marriage was not touched by a civil divorce.

I lived in Bonn in a rest-home run by sisters, and visited my wife at home every evening, and then returned to Bonn to spend the night. Only because throughout my life I had wanted to achieve final clarity about a fundamental legal question through our personal case, could I believe that I was allowed to demand this great personal relinquishment of my wife and myself.

Having waited for two years after having left the Old-Catholic Church, on October 23, 1984 we were divorced; as a result, I was accepted back into the Roman Catholic Church on November 24, 1984. It was a great pity, however, that the Vatican had *not* kept his word to readmit me to the priesthood, if I was divorced! The reason, I was told, was in fact, that I did not disavow my conviction of the divine right. Yet, I did take part in the theological discussion, also on other issues, such as in a debate about Karl Rahner's doctrine on Trinity and Christology, the authenticity of the Johannine writings etc. My voice was being heard again. There is still hope. St Paul says: "Hope does not allow us to be confounded" (Rom 5:5).

Chapter 9
The Mustard Seed Grows Into A Tree

Divorce and return to the Catholic Church were prerequisites for the desired continuing activity in favour of married priests. My time in the Old-Catholic Church had borne fruit. We had soon forgotten the tactical divorce. I moved into the matrimonial apartment as a lodger. Now, I could at least work within the Catholic Church, even if civilly divorced. Earlier, I had already noticed that Christianity frequently moves onward in such paradoxes.

The Worldwide Movement Of Married Priests

In the meantime, I had been integrated into the slowly growing movement of married priests since November 1982. I had long been surprised that the married priest brothers, for whom I had always fought, were largely unknown to me. All at once, I was invited to a meeting of "former priests" in the Cologne area. Five couples met near Duisburg. First contact was made.

In the course of the 1983, news spread that in September a "Synod of Married Catholic Priests and their Wives" was to take place in Chiusi, Italy. Because of the good experiences at the meeting in Duisburg, I decided to take part, despite initial scepticism. Some fifty delegates of different groups from Italy, Spain, France, Austria, Netherlands and Germany met at this synod held in a hotel in Tuscany, close to the health resort Chianciano Terme, and exchanged their experiences. Written comments, received from Brazil, the United States, South Africa and Hong Kong, made this meeting into an international agency for an estimated 80,000 married priests from all around the world. Meanwhile, the number of those who had retired from church service since the Second Vatican Council is of course even higher.

This large figure caused surprise with all, just as did the realisation that organised groups of "priests with family" – that is how the Italian and French groups called themselves – had already existed for a long time in the individual countries. The gathering had started simultaneously, almost everywhere, in the mid 1970s, about ten years after the possibility of dispensation from celibacy had been introduced by Pope John XXIII and his successor Paul VI in 1964. The first move had joined the individual priests in national groups. Now, a decade later, the groups joined at an international level.

The initiators of this "universal synod", as they called this meeting in contrast to regional meetings, were some Italian priest couples, who had gathered in the group OR.MA ("*Ordinazione e Matrimonio*"), this was also the title of their newsletter, or USFC ("*Unione Sacerdoti Familiari Cattolici*"), above all Paolo Camellini (died 2001) and his wife Carla from Reggio Emilia. The double courage to turn to their brothers all around the world, and to call their meeting a "synod" – a meeting of clergy who confess their belief –, goes back to a motivation by the Lord, as expressly stated in their OR.MA issue of January 1982. No doubt, the movement of gathering came from the Lord, as gathering is his activity: "Who does not gather with me, scatters" (Matt 12:30).

First Meeting In Chiusi

Those who met there were, for the most part, devout priests, who said their breviary every day. During the synod, a daily Mass was celebrated in a porch of the convention hotel, by a priest in office, who in each case had "accidentally" passed by.

We regarded the visit by a Consultor to the Congregation for the Clergy, Monsignor Mario Canciani, as a gift from heaven. He had become aware of the event through a newspaper report. He encouraged us with his sermon. The "via regia", he said, the "royal road" of obligatory celibacy (not the charisma, which will remain), must be given a danger sign: "Caution, defective road!," just as recently put up at the via Appia antica, which earlier bore the name "royal road."

With a respectful, yet clear appeal to Pope John Paul II and the Church, the Synod closed after a week, accompanied by the echo of the press, which was represented by the most important national and international papers: New York Times, Le Monde, Die Welt, La Stampa.

To my surprise, I was not unknown to several of the participants, because they had read my article in the international theological magazine "Concilium" of March 1980. So it happened that I was chosen to be a member of the international preparatory commission, which was to prepare the second, more important and bigger session of the Synod in 1985.

Preparation Of The Second Synod

At Pentecost 1984, the preparatory commission met in Paris for the first time. It comprised 16 members, among them an American, who had not spared the pain of the long flight. Because of my language skills and because of my public advocacy for the *ius divinum* of priests to marriage, the commission chose me as the coordinator, and a church journalist, the Dutchman Lambert van Gelder, he too versatile in foreign languages, as proxy.

Our team proved extraordinarily efficient. Out of the list of topics produced by the commission in Paris: "Compatibility of priesthood and marriage," "Divine right of priests to be married," "Indelible character of the ordained," "Right of the communities to a priest," "Pastoral reasons," etc., I made a ten page draft, which I then sent to the other members of the commission for correction. It was approved by the commission at the second session in Carpineti near Reggio Emilia, in November 1984.

In the meantime Lambert van Gelder had entered into extensive correspondence and, together with the Synod Secretary, Paolo Camellini, took on the organisational preparation. A group of women in Paris prepared a second text on "The Woman in the Church," the Spaniards a third one on "The base communities as the workplace of the married priest." They were approved, together with the by-laws of the synod, at the third plenary session of the commission, Easter 1985 in Marseilles.

Once more, I must thank God that, by his providence, I lived for the whole year of 1984 in the spiritual atmosphere of the rest-home in Bonn during the day. Because civil law demands a year of separation, before a divorce can take place, these circumstances were demanded. I was officially registered as unemployed, and therefore got support from the state, but also a small subsidy from the archdiocese Cologne. So, I was free to elaborate on the so-called "Scheme I. On compatibility of priesthood and marriage."

I was able to draft and improve the translation of the scheme into French together with the minister of the rest home, a Portuguese, who spoke French fluently. The Italian version was amended by guests from Rome. As to the English translation, the friend of a classmate of mine in the German Foreign Office was so kind as to help me: the Secretary of the British Embassy in person. Only the Spanish translation had to be prepared by a Spanish brother living in Marseilles.

This linguistic procedure, desired by our preparatory commission, had the invaluable advantage that our texts were immediately available for debate in the five languages of the synod. On the basis of these texts, later in 1986, the "International Federation of Married Catholic Priests" was established.

Another divine providence was crucial for the success of the synod. For years, a brother in Paris, who works in a dental laboratory, had spent his evenings at the computer and acquired considerable knowledge in the field of electronic word processing, at that time something rather new. He recognised the significance of his hobby for our business, and offered to write the text of the first scheme in all five languages on diskettes, so that the text could be immediately amended, according to the suggestions of the synod, and the printout submitted straight away to the public at end. And so it happened.

At the beginning of 1985, I undertook two trips, in order to fulfil the second task of the coordinator. This was to take up contact with the other groups in the world and to test the stand the Vatican would take with regard to the synod. I had earned the money for this by homework.

First, I flew to Chicago, where for a week I was a guest of Frank Bonnike's, leader of the group CORPUS, Corps of Reserve Priests United for Service. He introduced me to the local committees. His group alone then included 1,700 married priests, all of them ready to immediately take up their service again. 4,000 addresses, including cardinals and bishops who support them with money, were on their mailing list. All over North America, they estimated the married priests at approximately 17,000, almost one fourth of the 56,000 priests in office, whose average age is 52. The situation therefore was really dramatic already at that time.

Besides the great amount of information on the positive reception that married priests find in American society, I could regard it a success of the trip, that ten delegates from the United States registered for participation at the synod. Later, a Canadian also arrived.

The Stand By The Congregation For The Clergy

The next trip, in February 1985, took the three of us, van Gelder, Camellini and myself, by car to Rome. We first spoke with the leader of the largest Italian group VOCATIO, professor Gianni Gennari, who is now a journalist and later established excellent contacts for us with the international press. With the help of this group, we were able to hire the convention site, the study centre of the trade union C.G.I.L. in Ariccia in the Albanian mountains, 5 km from Castel Gandolfo. A visit there regulated the modalities. Above all, however, we spoke with the consultor of the Congregation for the Clergy, Mario Canciani, who had visited us in September 1983 in Chiusi. We had asked him by telephone if he could explore the stand of the Congregation with regard to us, because we had officially submitted our Scheme I there.

He informed the three of us in a detailed report in the sacristy of his parish in Rome, the basilica San Giovanni dei Fiorentini, next to the Tiber and close to the two bridges to the Vatican. The Congregation had received *exact instructions from the papal Secretariat of State* "to attribute no meaning and no official character" to our gathering. We could gather like every other group of Christians, nevertheless, the Congregation did not want to negotiate with the meeting as a whole, but only with individual priests about their concrete case. – The strategy was therefore the old Roman device *"Divide et impera"*!

If they accepted our demands, *"everything would collapse"*, *crollerebbe tutto*, they had said! Did the Congregation therefore regard the law of celibacy as the mainstay of the Church? Regarding the "convergent strategy" that they saw at work, they did not want to defer. We should not expect the Congregation to express itself, we should rather express ourselves, attest in fact that we have a "historical and a lived belief," that is, acknowledge tradition and love the present church. – The Congregation therefore was just waiting.

The Synod In Ariccia

Yet on several occasions, coordinator, proxy and secretary of the synod met in the Netherlands, Italy, or Bonn. The correspondence accumulated to five file folders. It turned out to be the most difficult task to persuade participants from Argentina and Brazil to travel to Ariccia, and to provide them with the necessary financial means. The Americans and the French helped, so finally one representative per country – with wives – were present. The printing of the texts and the composition of a whole Vademecum with information in the five languages was excellently procured at the expense of the Dutch by Lambert van Gelder. The rules of procedure for the synod were corrected for us by the Swiss lawyer Hans Urs Wili, with whom I had previously corresponded for years. So, at the end of July everything was prepared for the big event. One hundred and thirty delegates had registered, the press were invited.

The synod took place from August 25 to 31, 1985. None will ever forget the thunderous "*Veni Creator Spiritus*" sung in Latin, which opened the Synod. It was a twirling event of deafening noise in the foyers and breathless silence during the casting of votes, of exchange and discussion, joyful high spirits and tough confrontations, tamed by a moderate application of the by-laws, but united in the will to jointly express ourselves and give the world witness of our unbroken willingness to serve the Church.

Unanimous approval was granted to the five points of Scheme I, which were called "Catholic truths:" The press recognised this claim as being of doctrinal significance for the entire Church.

They were these:

1. Since all the sacraments of the Church derive from the same source, from Christ, priesthood and marriage cannot be incompatible, but must be able to join each other in the same Christian receiving them, in the Western as well as in the Eastern Church.

2. The right of the apostles and of all those who proclaim the Gospel to take along with them into the communities a sister as a wife, as formulated by Paul (1 Cor 9:5), is a complete power given to the apostles by Christ and therefore belongs to the unalterable *ius divinum*. It cannot be abrogated by the ecclesiastical legislator, because it is, moreover, a fundamental human right.

3. The so-called reduction of a priest to the lay state is impossible from the point of view of dogma; if it is done only because the priest wishes to receive the sacrament of marriage, it is an unjust measure.

4. Every community has the right to have the ministries necessary for itself and to present suitable candidates for these ministries. Furthermore the apostolic authority instituted by Christ has the duty to ordain by laying hands on those candidates whom the authority finds suitable.

5. Beside the theological reasons, there are also pastoral ones for the abrogation of the law of celibacy. The pastoral situation of the aging clergy, the empty seminaries, the orphaned communities asks for an amendment of the law of celibacy. The human maturity of priests not capable of celibacy would also no longer be hindered. Women would, in a certain way, have a say in the church. The reunification of the churches would be facilitated.

The commentary to these sentences documented at full length in the appendix of this book received only a relative majority. Others rather found themselves back in the additional commentaries of the Italians and Spaniards, which were based on the theology of the People of God and the base communities. The Women Scheme was reduced to four theses, and were accepted by the majority. The Base Communities Scheme in three theses was debated only briefly. An appeal to God's Church to accept married priests concluded the synod.

Press conferences were held at the beginning and end in Rome, in the Vatican owned hotel Columbus in the Via della Conciliazione. They provided a huge journalistic effect. Gianni Gennari had personally invited two hundred journalists by telephone to these conferences. In Ariccia, press, radio and television were present all the time. 65 articles were published in Italian newspapers alone in the week of the synod and the following. The press agency ADISTA collected them in a special dossier. Countless articles appeared in foreign countries.

Working at night, our computer expert completed the improved and approved texts, corrections were translated as an aside, and really: the last day we were able to hand over the print out of our first Synod document in five languages to the Vatican, and presented it to the press in the hotel Columbus immediately after.

Never has the Vatican pronounced a negative sentence on the document of the Synod, as it has done with regard to the issue of women priests in the document *Inter insigniores* dated May 22, 1994. This is indeed tantamount to an approval: *Qui tacet, consentire videtur*, silence gives consent. "The truth will set you free," is the promise of the Lord (Jn 8:32). We trust the Lord.

Chapter 10
A Victory Of The Right

I consider it a sign of divine providence that my personal case was taken up again after the Synod of Married Priests in Ariccia in 1985. It led to a kind of breakthrough with the Vatican authorities regarding the examination of the general question of the divine right of priests to get married.

Resumption Of The Case

At the end of the proceedings, the highest Vatican authority, the papal Secretariat of State, issued an opinion on 1 Cor 9:5. for the first time. For decades, the men in the Vatican had refused to accept even the question of whether the celibacy law – not the charismatic, free-chosen celibacy – was in conflict with the divine right of the Sacred Scripture. Again and again they had escaped to the "church law in force." The difference came after the synod. And it happened as follows.

The first victory in the struggle over the acknowledgment of the divine right of 1 Cor 9:5 was already accomplished in May 1985, when I asked the Cologne Curia: If it considered my sacramental emergency marriage of 1974 null and void (contracted before two witnesses, according to canon 1116 § 1 CIC/1983, given the 'moral' impossibility to find a priest assisting at the marriage), it should initiate a nullity suit against it.

After six months of negotiations, the General Vicar, whom I had asked on the phone, eventually told me: "We cannot bring such an action." —

"Thanks, I replied, this is what I wanted to know. Now, I'll move home to my wife again."

The excommunication they had threatened me with, if I were to resume living together with my wife, didn't arrive. The General Vicariate could not or did not want to bring the proof, that my marriage was null; but they could not punish me for a violation of the church law either.

After the Synod in Ariccia, the worldwide press echo and the silence of the Vatican with regard to it offered a new occasion to have the question about the validity of my sacramental marriage examined. Perhaps now it was possible to persuade Rome to decide on this pending personal case. The long favoured plan of a test case seemed to have a chance for realisation.

The whole process was possible only because I had not been dispensed from celibacy law. If I had done that, my marriage would have been declared valid only on the basis of a papal dispensation, that is, by *ecclesiastical* law. Yet because I had not been dispensed, I could maintain my conviction that our marriage was valid without the ecclesiastical special permit, on the basis of the prevailing *divine* right of the Sacred Scripture.

To avoid precisely the request for dispensation, we had consented to be divorced by a civil court. Therefore, I could now ask the question of whether our sacramental marriage, contracted in 1974 without dispensation, was "in order" without dispensation from the Holy See, because it was based on the divine right of 1 Cor 9:5. My whole life had focussed on this question. Now, amazingly, even if involuntarily, I got a positive answer from the Vatican.

Lawsuit Against The Law Itself

As a first step, in October 1985, I approached the Cologne Ecclesiastical Court for marriages, the so-called Officialate, a kind of diocesan tribunal. I asked it to check the validity of my marriage, which in 1974 I had contracted before two witnesses, on the basis of the divine right. Simultaneously, it should check whether the penalties, which the Cologne Curia had inflicted on us because of this marriage and because of the civil marriage, were unjustified and therefore null and void.

The answer by Professor Heinrich Flatten, a Cologne judge on marriage cases, already arrived a week later. What I wanted, he said, was not to verify the validity of my marriage, but essentially a declaration of nullity of the law, that is, of the ecclesiastical marriage-impediment for priests. I apparently wanted a judicial review of the law. "Judicial competence over the legislator," as exists in German civil law, meaning their Constitutional Court, "church law does not know," Professor Flatten declared in his letter dated November 6, 1985. Solely "the church legislator himself," that is "the highest authority in the Church, is responsible for such a decision," Flatten told me.

With this information from Professor Flatten, I had in my hands the admission ticket to the Roman authorities. I immediately sent my dossier to the Rota Romana. It forwarded it to the Congregation for the Doctrine of Faith in November of the same year. There I caught up with it, when I travelled to Rome myself in February 1986.

And now the astonishing fact happened: The secretary of the prefect of the Congregation for the Doctrine of Faith, Dr. Josef Clemens, after consultation with his chief, Cardinal Joseph Ratzinger, advised – not to drive home, as on earlier occasions – but to forward the dossier to the Pope in person. The reason: Because "he alone is above the law," that is, because the pope alone is not bound in obedience to the law, as even the Congregation for the Doctrine of Faith.

This was new to me. For, the Congregation for the Doctrine of Faith is indeed responsible for the examination of doctrinal questions, and the question of the exegesis of 1 Cor 9:5 is a doctrinal question. They now told me, it could not have been examined until now, because of the existing church law, which the Congregation has to obey! Only a bishop would have been able to submit the question to the agenda of the Congregation for examination. But, my bishop had constantly refused to do this for more than one year. My pending case, however, had to be adjudicated somehow. The only competent judge for it, I learned, is the Pope in person.

"The Pope Is Above The Law..."

Together with an accompanying letter written in Latin, in which my three questions were accurately formulated, I brought my dossier to the Vatican, on Monday, February 24, 1986. The letter was addressed to the Papal Secretariat of State.

The questions were: "Is 1 Cor 9:5 to be considered a divine right? Is my ecclesiastical emergency marriage, which is based on this divine right, to be regarded as valid? Are the penalties inflicted by my archbishop because of this marriage, null and void?" It also contained my article in the magazine "Concilium" from 1980, paper clips on the Synod of Ariccia, the comment by the Cologne Judge and a comment by the late Patriarch Athenagoras of Constantinopel regarding 1 Cor 9:5, which verse he also interpreted as the right of the apostles and their successors to live in marriage. My pointing to Athenagoras was destined to cut off the escape for the Vatican to say that even the Eastern Orthodox Church does not allow the marriage after ordination: This Church is apparently about to change this discipline.

On April 5, 1986, I received a message from the Substitute of the State Secretariat, archbishop Martinez, that my "question regarding ecclesiastical celibacy addressed to the Holy Father had arrived at the State-Secretariat," and is at present being considered and examined, *considerari et exquiri.*" Whoever knows the prehistory, the infinite efforts to reach such an examination, and the anguish, which preceded and followed our emergency marriage in 1974, will certainly imagine what this promise of examination, which included a judicial review, meant for me.

Nevertheless, I was once again at first awfully disappointed. On December 2, 1986 the Secretariat of State sent an answer, this time not signed by the Substitute, archbishop Martinez, the "third man" after the Pope and the Secretary of State, but by Monsignor Giovanni Battista Re, then Assessor of the State Secretariat. It was written in German.

The crucial information was: "The authentic interpretation of the biblical verse 1 Cor 9:5 contributes nothing to the canonical judgment on your priestly and matrimonial situation and is therefore not useful as a foundation for the three questions you submitted for examination: The apostle Paul in this verse merely claims to be equated in his state of life and in the opinion of the faithful with the other apostles. He points to the data seemingly prevalent at that time, namely that the apostles were *de facto* married. There is, however, obviously no discussion on the principal question of whether each human being has iure divino (on the basis of divine right) a *right* to get married, no more than about the question of whether any human being has the principal right to work or not to work (see 1 Cor 9,6-11)." – Let us examine the text.

The Discussion Is About Special Faculties Of The Apostles

The letter was called a "final comment." A decision, which I had asked for, therefore was not taken, just the opposite: the examination of the question was refused: "the authentic interpretation... contributes nothing to the canonical judgment." The Secretariat of State made known to me his *opinion*, regarding the content of 1 Cor 9:5, that we are not dealing with a *ius divinum* (divine right) for all humans.

The grave contradictions in this "opinion" are obvious. Paul, in the given verse, stresses his *licence* to take along a faithful as a wife, as the other apostles, the brethren of the Lord and Kephas do; the first word is therefore "*right*, entitlement" – *exousia*, or *potestas, licentia*, in the Greek original and in the official Latin translation. By contrast, the Vatican comment pretends to say, Paul does not deal with a "right", but only with the *actual state of life* of the other apostles, that is, their being *de facto* married. The apostle Paul, they say, wants to equate himself in the state of life with the other apostles. – Yet Paul *was not married* like the other apostles! In the state of life he was exactly *not* equal. Rather, Paul is stressing that he has the same *rights* as they have. He has the *right* to be married as they are, although he is not married *de facto*. Only in the right is he equal with the other apostles. He does, however, not take advantage of this right, as he emphasises somewhat later in the same context: "I have, however, not made use of any of such rights" (1 Cor 9:15).

Only his intention to stress his *rights* fits into the context of chapters 8 to 10, in which Paul wants to make plausible to the Corinthians precisely the renouncement of their rights, just like he had abstained from his rights. They shall renounce eating the meat sold on the market, which had previously been sacrificed to the idols in the heathen temples, although they actually have the right to eat it. For, idols don't exist, they are "null" (1 Cor 8:4 and 10:19). But because a "weak" brother, who still believes in the existence of idols, might take offense at the eating of his brother, the "stronger" brother should give up his right to eat the meat from the idol offerings, out of love for his brother. This is what Paul does with his rights as an *apostle* – these are not the rights of all Christians, such as the right to eat the meat of idol offerings, but special and central rights of office of the apostles: "Do I not have the right to eat and to drink?" *at the expense* of the communities, in which I announce the good news (1 Cor 9:4). Not each human being and not each Christian has this right, but only the preacher of the gospel! "Do I not have the right to take along a sister in faith as a wife, as the other apostles?", a wife which you then would have to nourish, together with me, as my assistant (1 Cor 9:5). "Or do alone Barnabas and I not have the right not to work?," that is, not to work with our own hands to earn our living, but to live on the donations of the communities (1 Cor 9:6). This is, of course, a special right of the apostles, not of every Christian faithful: "In the same way the Lord gave instructions that those *who preach the gospel* should get their living from the gospel" (1 Cor 9:14). Therefore the rights go back to the Lord, it is ius divinum. "I have, however, not made use of any of these things" (1 Cor 9:15). So the Corinthians should do, too (1 Cor 10:23-11:1).

What the verses 1 Cor 9:4-6 are all about, is therefore clearly the apostles' *rights*, which only and exclusively the apostles and the preachers of the gospel have been bestowed with, in fact by Christ, the Lord; therefore is it *ius divinum*, divine right, highest law in Canon law.

The answer from Rome mixes up the levels again and again. It denies that the text deals with *general* human rights, which is correct and which I had never asserted. It does, however, not take any notice of the fact that the text deals with *special rights of the apostles*. It denies that it deals with *rights* at all, and says that it deals with *facts*, while, in fact, Paul deals exclusively with rights, with the apostles' rights, not with his state of life. The Vatican answer disputes, that there is a discussion about the right to *work*, omits, however, that the text deals with the right of the apostles *not to work*, on which right the Church leaders live altogether, namely from donations or church taxes. The answer suggests that Paul speaks only about facts, not about divine right, however, it neglects that Paul stresses the fact that the right to live from the support of the communities derives *from the Lord*, who said: "Eat and drink, what they give you, for the worker deserves his wages." (Lk 10:7). We are therefore dealing with the Lord's instructions, which the Church itself calls divine right. We are dealing with facts only in this respect, namely that the *rest* of the apostles were actually married. That is what, after all, the Secretariat of State admits, and that is already a step forward. From this fact, however, Paul derives rights.

I discussed all this with Canon lawyers and New Testament scholars, and subsequently laid down a summary of it in several letters addressed to the Vatican. An answer never arrived.

"We Don't Want To Decide"

In April 1987, I travelled to Rome for another fourteen days, and asked for an audience with the Substitute, archbishop Martinez. After twelve days of waiting it was not granted, without indicating any reasons.

With three further letters dated May to July, I tried to persuade the Substitute to give a substantial answer. Dated July 4, 1987, I got the answer: "In answer to your question regarding the discipline, which you dispute, no other answer is possible than loyal acceptance."

On 13 July, I made a renewed objection, saying that I did not simply dispute the discipline but point to a collision between two disciplinary laws, namely the contradiction between the right to take along a wife according to 1 Cor 9:5, on one hand, which according to can. 199,1 of the Code of Canon Law 1983 is still *in force* in the Church today as a divine right, and, on the other hand, the celibacy law of can. 277. Furthermore, I said, I had asked for a decision on this collision to be taken by the Pope as the highest judge and legislator of the Church as from a Constitutional Court. I received the short answer from the Substitute Martinez, dated September 2, 1987, that "the Secretariat of State has nothing to add to what you have been told in the previous letters."

The pope, who alone is the top legislator and judge of the Church, has not yet been consulted up to the present day about the lawsuit against the norm itself. The State Secretariat is not a court. Only the Pope himself is "above the law", is therefore solely competent to pass a sentence on this question. So, I had been taught by the Congregation for the Doctrine of Faith.

On the Vatican's house phone, I was informed on August 23, 1987, by an official of the State Secretariat, Monsignor Paffhausen, regarding my request: "We *don't want* to judge, because the underlying question, of whether a divine right is given in 1 Cor 9:5, is so important that a bishop should submit it. The Church takes a decision on the meaning of a Bible verse only very rarely. If it does it at all, then only on request of a bishop, not on the request of a private person" (for the Vatican, it seems, a priest is just a private person!).

A Victory Of The Right

Here, it was clearly stated that the Papal Secretariat of State does *not want* to judge, and that it had not taken a decision so far. This answer did, of course, initially not satisfy me very much. But in reality, it contained the victory of the right - and for me.

On Easter Day 1987, at the feast of Jesus' resurrection, a canon of the CIC came to my mind, which declared our marriage valid even according to the current church law. I had asked the ecclesiastical judges from Cologne to Rome to pass a judgment on our sacramental marriage contracted in 1974. The highest judge in the Church, to which the Cologne judge had referred me, did not want to challenge the validity of our marriage. This means, however, it is to be regarded as valid according to current church law. A paragraph of the Code of canon law states: "The marriage enjoys legal favour; therefore, in the case of doubt, one must stand for the validity of the marriage, until the opposite is proven." (*Codex Iuris Canonici*, can. 1060; in the old Code of 1917 it was canon 1014). *Since not even the Vatican wants to prove the invalidity of our marriage, it is to be regarded as valid.* Therefore, the divine right of 1 Cor 9:5, the "licence to take along wives like the apostles," has won a victory through all the levels of church jurisdiction. The Vatican did not dare to decide against its validity, apparently for reverence of the divine right.

This interpretation doesn't go too far. I checked it several times with the Vatican authorities themselves. For, on December 13, 1987 my "doctor-father", the director of my doctoral thesis in Mainz, Rudolf Haubst, wrote the following: "In Rome, he said, one official who seems to be occupied with your case, told me: It is astonishing how you always bring new aspects and reflections into consideration. If you had only wanted the approval of your marriage in itself, everything would probably have been long regulated. Your principal position, however, seen from Rome, would set in motion many things not yet foreseeable."

In other words, I am embarrassing the Roman authorities with my arguments. They cannot refute them, for if they could, they would have done so long ago. On the other hand, however, they do not want to deal with my principal position on the biblical privilege, because they cannot measure the consequences.

If however a dire necessity exists to take a positive decision, because approximately 95,000 priests, one fifth of the Catholic clergy, have been dismissed from service for claiming the right to get married – which the pope himself called a "heavy wound at the life source of the church" and for which he ordered research to be done (*Acta Apostolicae Sedis* 72, 1980,1133), the church administration certainly cannot escape from the duty to decide, if it does not want to take on a severe responsibility.

In numerous letters addressed to the papal State Secretariat in the course of 1987, I always asked for such a decision. According to canons 1506 and 1507, the church is *obliged* to decide on a complaint on the invalidity or validity of a marriage. In 1988, I wrote nine letters to the General Vicar of Cologne, saying that I am living in a valid marriage as a priest, according to canon 1060, because the Vatican had not disputed its validity. Not before December 27 did he answer: "I beg your understanding, at the moment I cannot take up the matter, which you have been pursuing for years... We are helpless because of your lack of insight." Who actually has that lack?

Finally, I travelled to Rome, once more to see an assistant of Cardinal Ratzinger, the German prelate Helmut Moll, on August 31, 1988. I developed my opinion that my marriage as a priest had not been declared null by the State Secretariat; that it has therefore to be regarded as valid according to canon 1060. I told him, I was going to publish this victory of the right. Later, on September 3, I wrote a note for him with the content of our conversation, with the request to communicate it to Cardinal Ratzinger. He answered: "Ho preso atto, I have taken notice and am now informed". No contradiction came from the Vatican, as would have been a phrase like: "Your marriage is *not* valid!" or "Don't publish!" They didn't say that.

In September 1988, in fact as I had predicted, an article on my marriage was published in "Hoc Facite," a journal of the Italian priest Paolo Camellini, who had started the Synod. Once again, no objection or contradiction was heard from the Vatican.

On September 15, 1988 I wrote a long letter addressed to the new Substitute of the Secretariat of State, Edward Cassidy, and repeated my opinion that our marriage according to canon 1060 is valid and that all marriages of priests who appealed to the divine right of 1 Cor 9:5 therefore were valid. Again he did not protest. I added: "Allow me, please, another personal remark. I know from letters, which the prefect of the Congregation for the Doctrine of Faith, Cardinal Josef Ratzinger, wrote to my paternal friend Heinrich Spaemann in Ueberlingen and from which he has quoted the essential passages, without violating discretion, that Cardinal Ratzinger is convinced of the validity of my arguments, because he has not undertaken to refute them but has answered with the argument that changing the discipline would be a long-range decision, maybe the time was 'not yet' ripe for this, maybe the church 'still' ought to have the courage to hold on to this eschatological sign. The Cardinal, therefore, is not of the opinion that there are reasons which would force the Church by all means to hold on to celibacy for all priests. Only those who have the charisma can plausibly live the 'eschatological sign', of which he speaks." To this letter, as well, I got no answer, but also no contradiction, as if the Cardinal had never said those things I had quoted. Conclusion: The validity of my sacramental marriage has not been disputed by the Vatican.

I undertook a last attempt in August 1993. After legal consultation by the then Cologne judge on marriage cases, I brought the formal action to the Apostolic Signature, the highest Vatican court, to determine the constitutionality of the celibacy law, which disagrees with the divine right of the Sacred Scripture always in force. I said I was personally interested in the question, because I had been punished for appealing to the divine right and had been suspended from the priesthood, and would therefore have a right that the court received my complaint. On September 25, 1993 the Apostolic Signature answered: "The court is not competent to decide on the illegitimacy of a church law. Furthermore, according to church law (*Codex Iuris Canonici*, can. 333, § 3), no appeal is possible against laws enacted by the pope." Therefore, my complaint was refused.

This answer stimulates profound reflections: Does the pope also have a *legal* infallibility? Are questions about the divine law in the church irrelevant, only because the pope has enacted a different law? We are dealing with a right of the Sacred Scripture, which is acknowledged in the *Catholic Church of Eastern Rite*, therefore acknowledged also by the pope, because the CCEO – the Roman Catholic Code of the Eastern Churches' right, in force since October 18, 1990 – does not have a celibacy law! Why is it so difficult for the Catholic Western Church to acknowledge the divine right? Why can the Western Church not even acknowledge God's right to call whom he wants, in the West just like in the East? Is the pope, in other circumstances so courageous, afraid to take a "long-range decision," as Cardinal Ratzinger gave us to understand? Is this decision not really necessary at the beginning of the third millennium? In order to reverse the title "Alone against the Vatican" of the German edition of this book, at its end: It is not one man *alone*, who has fought this battle, but *all* the dispensed priests degraded to the lay state; besides, we did not fight *against* but *for* the Vatican, for the church: the good fight of the faith (1 Tim 6:12), for the benefit of the communities, who are waiting for priests in order to be able to serve them.

In any case, I believe I have done what I was commissioned to do, through the provisional victory of the right in Rome. Perhaps, I have already received this commission on my birthday, by pope Gregorius VII, and even more so by the Lord in heaven. Since that Easter 1988, when I pondered the Vatican's "We don't' want to decide", I have felt liberated from the permanent pressure which my life-long problem exercised on me, and I sense a complete inner peace, which contrasts with the continuous tension of the years since 1952. Now, I can finally work productively in theology. The first fruit of this new activity was, in 1988, a book, which became the basis for further theological commissions. It wants to lead to "Jesus Christ, a reality," not a fairy-tale. He has given proof of that reality in my life as well.

The final stage of my career – at least so far – was the appointment as an assistant professor for Bible Studies at the University of Koblenz. For twelve years from 1995 to 2006, I was able to pass on my love for the New Testament to future teachers of religion in primary and secondary schools. I did not stop writing letters to Cologne and the Vatican, yet these could not touch my inner peace. I am now waiting for the success of all the arguments gathered in this book.

The conclusion from all the efforts in my battle for the right of a Catholic priest to be married, is this: Every priest can enter a sacramental marriage referring himself to 1 Cor 9:5. Rome will not declare such a marriage invalid, because the Petrine office cannot decide against the divine right, and has not done so in my case.

And the conclusion for laypeople is: If priests who are not endowed by God with the charism of celibacy have the right to be married, then the laity has the right to have married priests, as well in the East of the Catholic Church, as in the Latin speaking West. 45.000 married priests are waiting to be reinstalled, and in the future no shortage of priests would ever occur.

Appendix

General Synod of Married Catholic Priests and their Wives

Second Session 1985

First Document

Compatibility of Priesthood and Marriage

The married Catholic bishops and priests represented in this synod and their wives, on the basis of the Church's decisions of faith, give unanimously testimony of the following Catholic truths:

1. Since all the sacraments of the Church derive from the same source, from Christ, priesthood and marriage cannot be incompatible, but must be able to join each other in the same Christian receiving them, in the Western as well as in the Eastern Church.

2. The right of the apostles and of all those who proclaim the Gospel to take along with them into the communities a sister as wife, as formulated by Paul (1 Cor 9:5), is a complete power given to the apostles by Christ and therefore belongs to the unalterable *ius divinum*. It cannot be abrogated by the ecclesiastical legislator, because it is, moreover, a fundamental human right.

3. The so-called reduction of a priest to the lay state is impossible from the point of view of dogma, if it is done only because the priest wishes to receive the sacrament of marriage, it is an unjust measure.

4. Every community has the right to have the ministries necessary for itself and to present suitable candidates for these ministries. Furthermore the apostolic authority instituted by Christ has the duty to ordain by the laying on of hands those candidates whom the authority finds suitable.

5. Beside the theological reasons there are also pastorals ones for the abrogation of the law of celibacy.

I a) The priests in nearly all countries are old.

b) Seminaries remain empty, except in some few countries

c) Up to one third of Catholic parishes have no pastor of their own.

d) One In five Latin Catholic priests have married.

e) The papal dispensations for converted pastors to remain married as priests have created inequality and legal insecurity.

II a) The evidence of chosen celibacy on one hand and of matrimonial union on the other would be clearer and more striking.

b) The human maturity of priests who have no charismatical vocation to celibacy would be possible.

c) Married people would be represented in the leadership of the church, so that the interests of all might equally be respected.

d) Women could take part in the decisions of the church, as is widely accepted in secular society.

e) Priests could better take part in the life of the faithful.

f) The clandestine partnerships between priests and women, which are unworthy to human dignity and which do harm specially to the women, would cease.

g) The desired approachment to the other Christian confessions who all admit the married minister, would be greatly facilited.

Ariccia, 30 August 1985. Giustino Zampini, president, +Jerónimo Podestà, vice-president, Paolo Camellini, secretary, Heinz-J. Vogels, coordinator prep. comm.

Commentary

Immediately after the unanimous vote for the first document and for pluralism, the following commentary was accepted by the largest number of votes as a legitimate expression of our believe.

1. Since all the sacraments of the Church derive from the same source, from Christ, priesthood and marriage cannot be incompatible, but must be able to join each other in the same Christian receiving them, in the Western as well as in the Eastern Church.

The II. Lateran Council (1139) condemned in canon 23 as heretics those "who condemn the sacraments of the body and blood of Christ, the baptism of children, the priesthood and the others ecclesiastical orders and the legitimate conjugal union" (1). The Council thus gives the same rank to priesthood and marriage. It is therefore impossible for a Catholic to deny the sacramental dignity of matrimony. It is founded on the human dignity of woman which is equal to that of man, accorded to both by the Creator (Gen 1:27), and on the complementary nature of the two human beings.

The Council of Trent (1545-1561) determined that "all the seven sacraments are instituted by Christ" (2) and it stressed especially with regard to matrimony: "It is Christ himself, the creator and perfector of the venerable sacraments, who merited for us through his passion the grace which sanctifies the couple" (3). Nowhere is asserted an incompatibility of priesthood and matrimony; on the contrary the Vatican Council II (1965) states explicitly that "perfect abstinence is not required by the nature of the priesthood, as is shown by the practice of the early church and the tradition of the oriental churches, where there are priests of great merits in the conjugal state" (4).

In opposing these conciliar statements the 7th canon of the II. Lateran Council prohibited marriage to all priests of the Latin rite from the year 1139 on, by declaring future unions null and void, and separating existing ones, in clear contradiction to the commandment of Christ: "What God has joined together, let not man put asunder" (Matt 19:6). The particular reason given by the Council for the prohibition of marriage was: "in order that the God pleasing purity might spread among ecclesiastical persons and sacred orders" (5), which represented an implicit condemnation of marriage as being impure, and thus a contradiction to the Council's own doctrine uttered in canon 23 quoted above. Canon 7, derived from the spirit of the monastical reform of Cluny and on which all the future celibacy legislation of the Latin Church was built, is thus in contradiction to the dogma about the sacramental dignity of marriage; by seeking to divorce existing marriages, it is in contradiction to the divine commandment of indissolubility defined by the Council of Trent (6); finally, it is also in contradiction to the compatibility of priesthood and marriage which was explicitly stated only by the II. Vatican Council, but was always practised by the Catholic church, especially in the East.

For, until the 12th century the marriage of priests was the rule, along with spontaneous renunciation of marriage, in the Latin church of the West also. This fact is attested by cardinal Humbert of Silva Candida, legate of pope Leo IX, during the negotiations in Constantinople which led to the great schism of 1054. He wrote to Niketas, abbot of Studiou monastery: "The Roman Church only allows the clergy of lowers orders to marry a virgin wife with a priest's benediction. If someone wants to ascend from these orders to subdeaconate (deaconate, presbyterate or episcopate), he may not do so without the prior agreement of his wife that their corporal marriage shall thenceforth become a spiritual one" (7).

Although, in that way, abstinence *in* marriage was required from the Western priests, while in the East the legitimate conjugal rights of the priests remained respected (8), both parts of the church agreed that priests of all ranks might *be* married, that is live in the life-long community of husband and wife. As for the justification of this practice, Cardinal Humbert as well as the monk Niketas based themselves on the apostolic canon 5 (of the 4th century): "No bishop, priest, deacon may dismiss his wife from his care on the pretext of piety" (9), and on the usage of the apostles themselves mentioned by Paul: "Do we not have the right to take along with us a sister (in Christ) as wife, as the other apostles and the brothers of the Lord and Cephas?" (1 Cor 9:5). The last passage of Humbert's letter with the two quotations was inserted by Gratian into his 'Decretum Gratiani' and thus remained part of the Corpus Juris Canonici, in force until 1918 (10). The prohibition of marriage for priests uttered by the II. Lateran Council therefore placed itself in plain contradiction to the well known tradition of the first millennium of the undivided church, before 1054, when married priests were admitted. The compatibility of both sacraments thus is attested by the tradition of the West as well as of the East.

Law must respect the rights of those subject to it and must not restrict them without sufficient reason. The reason why the dogmatic and legal compatibility of marriage and priesthood was annulled, namely that purity could only be achieved through celibacy, is dogmatically and morally unjustifiable. Therefore the law is illegitimate.

Another contemporary reason for the law seems to have been the endeavour to avoid waisting and splitting of church benefices through inheritance by the priest's children, as well as to prevent the possibility of sons inheriting their father's profession, both possibilities connected with the feudal system of the Middle Ages when a landowner could appoint a priest to his own church and present him to the bishop for ordination. This made it possible for persons without a vocation from God to enter the clerical state. Even if such reasons did exist then and might have given some justification to the law, conditions have changed considerably in the meantime. The material welfare of priests is generally no longer provided by benefices, but by a regular salary or by gifts from the faithful, according to the customs of the different countries; and the approbation of candidates to priesthood is decided by the bishop after consultation with the seminary professors. All the historical reasons for the introduction of the law thus no longer apply.

The Church of this century has found a new and enriched understanding of the sacrament of marriage. This should have its effect on the policy of celibacy. A married priesthood is endowed with charisms lacking in a celibate priesthood. Family life sensitises a priest to pastoral concerns in a different manner. Married people find in a married priest someone who seems capable of understanding them better. Married people see in the married priest someone who lives their own life style, someone whose celebration of the Eucharist ennobles all married life in a special way.

Therefore this assembly regards the law of mandatory celibacy which is imposed on the priesthood in the Western Church only, as illegitimate both from dogmatic and legal points of views, and pleads in favour of its formal abolition.

The order in which the two sacraments are received, need not be of importance. The fact that even in the Eastern Church marriage after ordination is not allowed, has been judged unjust in our time by the late patriarch Athenagoras of Constantinople. He proposed the alteration of that law to the future panorthodox council which not yet has taken place. For that purpose he, too, referred to the verse 1 Cor 9:5 (11).

2. The right of the apostles and of all those who proclaim the Gospel to take along with them into the communities a sister as wife, as formulated by Paul (1 Cor 9:5), is a complete power given to the apostles by Christ and therefore belongs to the unalterable *ius divinum*. It cannot be abrogated by the ecclesiastical legislator, because it is, moreover, a fundamental human right.

New Testament scholars today are unanimous that the "sister" in the Pauline text is a sister in Christ and the "woman" is the wife which "the other apostles (12), the brothers of the Lord", Simon and Jude Thaddeus (13), "and Cephas", Peter (14), actually did take with them and which Paul and Barnabas might have taken with them, if they had wanted (15). The most ancient Fathers of the Church, Tertullian, Clement of Alexandria, Hilary of Poitiers and the young Jerome, translated the Greek word for woman by "uxorem", wife (16). The elder Jerome, obviously under the influence of abstinence regulations issued by pope Siricius (17), preferred the translation "mulierem", woman (18), which was adopted by the later Fathers. In the Middle Ages the two words *sororem* and *mulierem* were inverted in some manuscripts: mulierem sororem circumducere, to take with us a woman as sister, so that the meaning of the verse was hidden. This altered text was printed in the Vulgate edition issued under pope Clement VIII. in 1592 and remained the official text of the Western Catholic Church for almost 400 years. That is why the real significance of the text remained unknown.

The right of the Apostles to be married, according to this text, is not merely a natural and human right, guaranteed by the Bible (Gen 1:28; 2:18.24; Matt 19:4-6; 1 Cor 7:9.28.39), it is in addition to that a right attached to the office of the apostles to be accompanied by their wife. The natural and human right alone forbids a human legislator, be it even the Church, to establish an absolute impediment to marriage for priests. Ordination is the only absolute matrimonial impediment in purely ecclesiastical law; the others are relative concerning those persons with whom a Christian may not contract marriage. Imposing an absolute impediment for priests to marry, as was done by the II. Lateran Council, without taking into consideration the liberty of the priests, is equal to "forbidding marriage", which the I. Epistle to Timothy calls a "doctrine of demons" (4:1), because "every creation of God is good and nothing is to be rejected that is taken with gratitude; it is sanctified by God's word and prayer" (4:4-5). At least today when the Church is defending human rights in all fields, it is inconsequent for the Church not to allow use to be made of the right to marriage within itself.

But the full power of the apostles to take along wives on the missionary journeys and into the communities is more than a natural right, it belongs to the official rights that were Paul's and the other apostles' because they were apostles, and were granted to them by the Lord himself who called them to follow him (1 Cor 9:1-3). The other rights mentioned by Paul are "the right to eat and to drink" what the communities gave them (9:4) and "not to work" by their own hands to gain their living (9:6); for "in the same way the Lord commanded that those who proclaim the Gospel should live by the Gospel" (9:14). Paul is thinking of the Lord's words: "Eat and drink what they provide, for the laborer deserves his wages" (Lk 10:7; Matt 10:10).

The more general right of the apostles and of all preachers of the Gospel to accept maintenance from the faithful for whom they work, according to these scriptural texts, is a divine right granted to them by Christ the Son of God. Therefore it is of the same unalterabie and supreme validity as the full powers on which Peter and his successors rely in governing the universal church (Matt 16:18; Jn 21:15-17) and the bishops in ruling their dioceses (Matt 18:18; Jn 20:21; Acts 20:28). The right of receiving maintenance applies to the wives of the apostles, too, as is stressed by Paul when he called the right of bringing them a "full power" (exousia) like the other apostolic rights. Full power in the whole New Testament is a standard expression for permission derived from God, a technical term for *ius divinum* (divine right) (19). Consequently the right to bring wives into the communities is also a divine right, attached to the office of apostolate, because the apostles could demand the maintenance from the communities for their wives, too. No human law is able to take away this divine right from proclaimers of the Gospel, for *ius divinum* according to its nature cannot be abrogated by the church; it is rather the basis of all ecclesiastical law (20).

Thus the priests have a justified claim towards the papal authority to declare null and void the law of celibacy, which does not oblige only those called charismatic but all priests to the single life, as being contradictory to divine law, both natural and apostolic as formulated by St. Paul, and to restore the ecclesiastical validity of the divine right to take wives.

3. The so-called reduction of a priest to the lay state is impossible from the point of view of dogma, if it is done only because the priest wishes to receive the sacrament of marriage, it is an unjust measure.

The Council of Trent determined that the sacerdotal ordination, like baptism and confirmation, "impresses an indelible seal" (21) in the Christian, as is said in the II. Letter to Timothy: "The gift of grace which is in you through the laying on of my hands" (1:6), and it threatened with banishment anyone who should say that "a man once ordained priest might become layman again" (22). This means that the power of consecration rests upon the priest forever; only the jurisdictional power may be taken away from him by law or judgment. Now, the present legislation of the church grants the dispensation from celibacy only in connection with the "reduction to the laical state" (23). If a believer is in danger of death, the "reduced" priest may always lawfully use his spiritual powers (24). But otherwise he cannot even make use of the laical faculties in liturgy and proclamation of the word (25).

The so called "reduction to the state of laymen" is, according to the quoted words of the Council of Trent, impossible, and even more: threatened by the Council with excommunication. In fact the reduction of a priest only because he wishes to receive a sacrament, that of matrimony, is unjust, both towards the Lord who has called the priest to his service, and towards the community which is deprived of a pastor, and to the priest himself who has not committed a fault deserving the degradation. Otherwise reduction to the lay state or, according to the new Code, loss of clerical state, is foreseen by the law only for the most serious transgressions of a priest (26). He who begs for dispensation from the law of celibacy, however, has done nothing but to come to the conclusion - because of the "difficulties" acknowledged by the Congregation of Faith in its document of 1980 (27) - that he has not received the charism of celibacy from the Lord, in spite of all his prayers as recommended by the Church (28); for really "not all can grasp this thing, but only those to whom it is given" (Matt 19:11; 1 Cor 7:7). "The sacraments are there for men" (sacramenta propter homines): it is a contradiction to this pastoral rule, if a Christian, be he priest or not, is punished by the loss of his vocation and his honour when receiving a sacrament (29).

The ecclesiastical legislator tries to justify the punishment on the ground of a breach of faith by the priest against his vocation and the obligations attached to it (30). Here a distinction must be made. There is a vocation to priesthood (Hebr 5:4) and the vocation to celibacy (Matt 19:11; 1 Cor 7:7). Many priests who have married, wanted to be faithful to their vocation of spreading the Gospel and serving the communities. No one has left his ministry voluntarily. They have instead been forced to do it by order of the ecclesiastical law which grants dispensation to marry only if the priest renounces his office. But these priests begged for dispensation of celibacy, because they had become aware that they did not have the second vocation, the one to celibacy; for the life in celibacy, as is recognised by the II. Vatican Council, is not possible without the charism, the special gift from God, of which the Lord speaks. The Council affirms that one can only "choose celibate life" by means of "a vocation of grace" (31), that "the Father" must "give the vocation to celibacy" (32), that celibacy is a "great gift granted by the Father" (33). He who receives this gift from God, will certainly observe celibacy voluntarily and spontaneously, even without a law. But he who does not receive the gift, cannot be forced by law to have it, since God cannot be compelled, even by prayer, to give it. For this person the law cannot be fulfilled. And only the priest himself can ultimately decide if he has got the charism or not.

Nowhere does the Holy Scripture say that the charism of celibacy is given to all priests. On the contrary Paul says that the apostles, after having left their wives to follow Christ (Matt 19:27), took them later with them on the missionary journeys (1 Cor 9:5), and the Pastoral Letters require only that "the priest, bishop, deacon be the husband of only one wife (or once married)" (1 Tim 3:2.12; Tit 1:6). From that one can see that the vocation to priesthood and that to celibacy do not always coincide in the same person. On the contrary, a real vocation of a considerable number of priests to marriage does exist, which is not a defect but a different gift from God (1 Cor 7:9), a diverse state of evangelical perfection (Eph 5,21-33). This fact is confirmed by the II. Vatican Council when speaking of the "priests of great merits in the conjugal state" (34), in the oriental churches. Consequently the celibacy law of the Western Church which only admits celibates to priesthood, is an unjust law, because it contradicts the teaching and the rules of the New Testament regarding the different vocations of God for his priests, and because it offends the principle of equality in law which requires that the admission to Priesthood be ruled by the same conditions in East and West.

Thus priests without the charism and who therefore want to receive the sacrament of marriage do not commit any breach of faith. On the contrary, one must admit that the legislator of the Latin Church, disregarding the variety of vocations from God for his priests, has obliged all of them, since 1139, to do something impossible for those who haven't got the charism. According to the principles of morality and canon law an unjust and impossible law cannot have force in the *forum internum* of conscience (35). For those who find out that they have not been granted the gift of celibacy, the natural right of the Genesis (1:28) and the divine right of the apostles (1 Cor 9:5) to be married remains valid.

For all these reasons this synod addresses the urgent request to the ecclesiastical legislator to abrogate formally in the *forum externum* a law which cannot be observed by many priests and which is unjust; that he may take away the discriminations linked to the dispensation from celibacy, and issue new just conditions of admission to the sacerdotal ministry, for the life of celibate priests and the state of the married clergy.

As Iong as a married priesthood is not introduced into the Latin Church, we expect the Pope to quickly grant dispensations from the obligation of celibacy requested by certain priests and to do so in a manner that respects human dignity.

4. Every community has the right to have the ministries necessary for itself and to present suitable candidates for these ministries. Furthermore the apostolic authority instituted by Christ has the duty to ordain by the laying on of hands those candidates whom the authority finds suitable.

The Code of Canon Law accords to the faithful "the right of receiving from their spiritual pastors help from the spiritual goods of the Church, especially the word of God and the sacraments" (36), and it states on Eucharist: "Any baptised person who is not prevented by law, can and must be allowed to receive the holy communion" (37). These rights cannot be realised without a sufficient number of priests. Normally the proclamation of the Word of God and the administration of the sacraments are realised in the local communities. Therefore these need pastors.

Paul the apostle "installed presbyters in each community" (Acts 14:23) and he ordered the same to be done by his disciple Titus: "For that purpose I left you in Crete that you may install presbyters in each town, as I told you to do" (Tit 1:5). From that it is clear that he did not only care for whole regions by the appointment of bishops, like Titus for Crete and Timothy for Ephesus (1 Tim 1:3), but also for the little local communities by giving them priests. The same duty is inherited by the successors of the apostles, the pope and the bishops of today. Such presbyters were always, and could be, as much celibates as married men. The number of celibate priests is not sufficient in many countries and a great number of priests are compelled to abandon their ministry because of the dispensation rules on celibacy. So the main reason for the shortage of priests is to be seen in the law of celibacy. Indeed there are sufficient students of theology and *"viri probati"* (approved men), who are prepared to accept priestly ministry without obligation to celibacy. That is why the lack of priests is another motive for the authorities to annul the law of celibacy, because it contradicts the pastoral principles of the apostles, the signs of the time and the needs of the people of God, and to admit married men as well as celibates to priesthood, in order that the number of "the workers in the harvest of the Lord" may increase (Matt 9:37; Lk 10:2).

The right of the communities to have a priest with them, is fundamental and essential, even necessary for the celebration of eucharist, therefore based on the divine law (Lk 22:19; Acts 2:42.46; 1 Cor 11:23). The ecclesiastical conditions of admission to the sacerdotal ministry are temporary, changeable and based on purely human law. In case of a conflict the human law must give way to the divine law.

The same principle ought to rule the dismissal of a priest from his ministry. Mere rules of discipline must not detain a priest from realising his fundamental duties accepted with the ordination, that is the spreading of the Gospel and the administering of the sacraments. Then discipline would lose its character of mere regulation. Rules of discipline must not induce a priest to infidelity towards the commission received from the Lord.

We encourage Christian communities to accept married priests and to ask their bishops to send married priests into their parishes, and to support them in their ministries, all of this in accord with the previous arguments.

5. Beside the theological reasons there are also pastorals ones for the abrogation of the law of celibacy.

I a) The priests in nearly all countries are old.

b) Seminaries remain empty, except in some few countries

c) Up to one third of Catholic parishes have no pastor of their own.

d) One in five Latin Catholic priests have married.

e) The papal dispensations for converted pastors to remain married as priests have created inequality and legal insecurity.

II a) The evidence of chosen celibacy on one hand and of matrimonial union on the other would be clearer and more striking.

b) The human maturity of priests who have no charismatical vocation to celibacy would be possible.

c) Married people would be represented in the leadership of the church, so that the interests of all might equally be respected.

d) Women could take part in the decisions of the church, as is widely accepted in secular society.

e) Priests could better take part in the life of the faithful.

f) The clandestine partnerships beetween priests and women, which are unworthy to human dignity and which do harm specially to the women, would cease.

g) The desired approachment to the other Christian confessions who all admit the married minister, would be greatly facilited.

More important than these pragmatical reasons is the will of the Lord who on the one hand has explicitely said that "not all are capable" of celibacy (Matt 19:11), not even all priests, and on the other has accorded through the words of Paul to the proclaimers of the word the right of taking a wife into the communities (1 Cor 9:5). These, in turn, have the duty of giving the preachers to eat and to drink (9:4-6), in order that the preaching of the Kingdom of God may be assured.

Nevertheless the individual priest is free to renounce his right of maintenance from the faithful, as Paul did (1 Cor 9:15; 2 Thess 3:8f), and to live from his own work in a civilian profession. Thus he could serve the communities on Sundays "gratuitously" like Paul (1 Cor 9:18), a view of a priest which is often realised today: the priest-worker (38).

Notes:

1. Denzinger 367, Denzinger-Schönmetzer 718.

2. D 844, DS 1601.

3. D 969, DS 1799.

4. Vatican Council II, Presbyterorum Ordinis 16.

5. Conciliorum Oecumenicorum Decreta (Basilea 1962) 174: «Ut autem lex continentiae et deo placens munditia in ecclesiasticis personis et sacris ordinibus dilatetur, statuimus, quatenus episcopi, presbyteri, diaconi...et monachi..., qui sanctum transgredientes propositum (var. lect.: praeceptum) uxorem sibi copulare praesumpserint, separentur. Huismodi namque copulationem, quam contra ecclesiasticam regulam constat esse contractam, matrimonium non esse censemus."

6. D 977, DS 207.

7. Migne, PL 143,999D; PG 120,1037D.

8. Canons of the Trullanum in 692; in the Decretum Gratiani D.31 c.13 (Friedberg I, 114).

9. PL 143,981D and 997D; PG 1201,1019D and 1035D. Cf. Didaskalia et Constitutiones Apostolorum, ed. F.X. Funk (Paderborn 1905) 564.

10. D.31 c.11 (Friedberg I,114).

11. O. Clement, Dialoghi con Atenagora (Turino 1972) 191: "La riforma che consentirebbe al prete di sposarsi dopo l'ordinazione"; 192: "San Paulo ci dice che Pietro e gli alteri apostoli avevano ognuno la propria compagna."

12. As e.g. Philip, who had three daughters: Eusebius, Hist. eccl. III,31,2-3.

13. Jude Thaddeus, had two grandsons: Eusebius, Hist. eccl. III,20,1-5.

14. Peter's mother-in-law, whom Jesus cured, is mentioned Mk 15:30; Matt 8:14; Lk 4:38.

15. "Uxores circumducere" in Biblische Zeitschrift 3 (1959) 94-102; Concilium 133 (3/1980) 84-92.

16. Tertullianus, Exhort. cast. 8 : CSEL 70,141; Clement of Alex., Paidagogos II,1,9: PG 8,392B; Hilary of Poitiers, Tract. in Ps. 118 Nun 14: CSEL 22,483,8-17; Jerome, Advers. Helvid. 11: PL 23,194B (204A); Jerome, Epist. 22,20: CSEL 54,171, dating from the early year 384.

17. Epistola ad Himerium dated 10.2.385: D 89. The pope calles it "obscoenis cupiditatibus inhiare", that priests "post longa consecrationis suae tempora tam de coniugibus propriis, quam etiam de turpi coitu sobolem procreaverunt". The text was not inserted into the new edition of Denzinger-Schönmetzer: the motive of impurity in marriage is too evident.

18. Jerome, Advers. Jovinian. 1,26: PL 23,245B (257A), dating from the year 393.

19. Cf. Theol. Wörterbuch zum NT II,563.

20. Cf. can.6 n.6 CIC/1917; can. 22 CIC/1983 and the commentaries and manuals of the CIC.

21. D 852, DS 1609.

22. D 964, DS 1774.

23. Normae ad apparandas... causas reductionis ad statum laicalem cum dispensatione ab obligationibus cum Sacra Ordinatione connexis: AAS 63 (1971) 303-308. Normae procedurales de dispensatione a sacerdotali caelibatu: AAS 72 (1980) 1136f. The rescript of dispensation by the Congregation of Faith «amplectitur inseparabiliter amissionem status clericalis».

24. Can. 976 CIC/1983.

25. Normae 1971 (AAS 63,308) Forbidden to the reduced priest are all liturgical functions, preaching, pastoral ministry, teaching catechism, management of catholic schools, except teaching catechism in secular schools. The same is prescribed by the rescript of the Congregation of Faith in 1980 (Annex to AAS 72,1137).

26. Can. 1367,1370,1387,1395 § 2 CIC/1983: Apostasy, attack against the pope, violation of the sacramental seal, seduction of minors. Cf. can. 291f CIC/1983: amissio status clericalis, where no difference is made between loss of clerical state by penalty and by dispensation.

27. AAS 72 (1980) 1133: «Difficultates, quas praesertim ultimorum annorum decursu sacerdotes experti sunt, effecerunt ut haud parvus numerus eorum postulaverint dispensationem ab obligationibus peculiarique modo dispensationem a caelibatu."

28. D 979, DS 1809; Vaticanum II, Presbyterorum Ordinis 16 III.

29. Regula Iuris IX in VI.to: «Sine culpa non est aliquis puniendus" (Friedberg II,1122).

30. AAS 72 (1980) 1133: «Christifideles expectant - addit Sanctitas Sua -, exemplum bonum ac testimonium fidelitatis erga vocationem usque ad mortem». Litterae Apostolicae «Reconciliatio et Paenitentia» dated Dec. 21 1984, n.34: «Christians whose situation is in contradiction to their obligations voluntarily accepted before God and the Church»; «priests who don't observe their severe obligations accepted with the ordination and who therefore are in an irregular situation».

31. Presbyterorum Ordinis 16 I: "ex dono gratiae coelibatum eligunt."

32. Ibid. 16 III: "Donum coelibatus liberaliter a Patre dari".

33. Ibid. 16 III: "praeclarum illud donum, quod a Patre sibi datum est"; the Council quotes Matt 19:11.

34. Presbyterorum Ordinis 16 I.

35. Regula iuris VI in VI.to: "Nemo potest ad impossibile obligari" (Friedberg II,1122)

36. Can. 213 CIC/1963; cf. can. 682 CIC/1917.

37. Can. 912 CIC/1983, cf. can. 843 § 1.

38. Cf. our synodal document III: "Married priests faithful to their service in the Church". Cf. can. 288 CIC/1983: The permanent deacons, may they be married or not, are allowed to exercise a secular profession.

www.ingramcontent.com/pod-product-compliance
Lightning Source LLC
LaVergne TN
LVHW061035070526
838201LV00073B/5044